CRUISING IN TI
MALDIVE
DIVING GUIDE

SWAN·HILL
PRESS

CRUISING IN THE
MADIVES
DIVING GUIDE

Text and photographs
Claudio Cangini

Editorial production
Valeria Manferto De Fabianis
Laura Accomazzo

Graphic design
Anna Galliani

Illustrations of the dives
Cristina Franco

Translation
Studio Traduzioni Vecchia, Milano

*The Publisher would like to thank Ms Naseema Mohamed
and Mr Hassan Ahmed Haniku for their precious help.
The Author would like to thank Ms Nadia Alzani for her precious
assistance.*

*1 A boat lies
anchored in the
tranquil waters in
the lagoon of
Bandos, an island
in the North Malé
Atoll. By mooring
near the resort, it is
usually possible to
disembark and
make use of
village facilities.*

*2-3 A dense
school of batfish
(Platax
orbicularis)
swims tranquilly
in the open water.
These fish usually
live in pairs near
the reef and are
easy to approach.*

*6-7 Several
surgeonfish
(Acanthurus
xanthopterus)
move rapidly near
the seabed. Note
the two horny
blades on the
caudal peduncle
that the fish uses
for self-defense.*

© 1996 White Star S.r.l.

First Published in the UK in 1998
by Swan Hill Press, an imprint
of Airlife Publishing Ltd.

British Library Cataloguing in
Publication Data
A catalogue record for this book is
available from the British Library

ISBN 1 85310 942 8

Printed in April 1998 by
Grafedit, Bergamo, Italy.
Colour separation by Cliché Offset,
Milan, Italy.

Contents

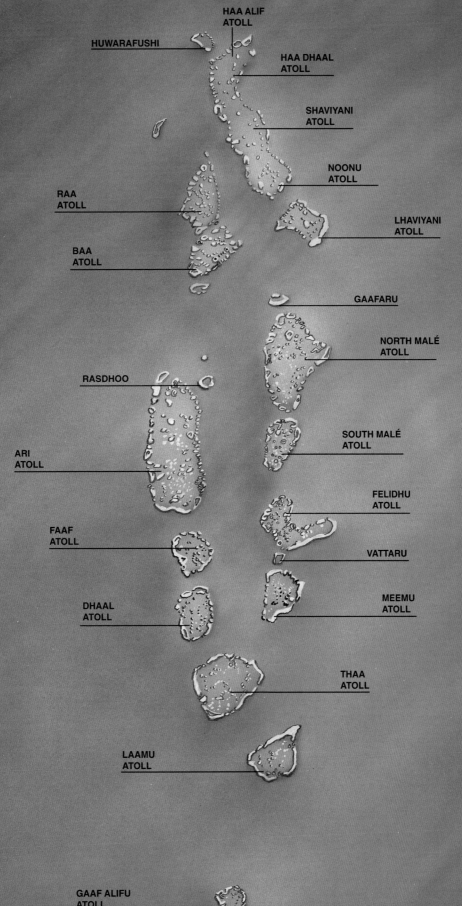

HAA ALIF
ATOLL

HUWARAFUSHI

HAA DHAAL
ATOLL

SHAVIYANI
ATOLL

NOONU
ATOLL

RAA
ATOLL

LHAVIYANI
ATOLL

BAA
ATOLL

GAAFARU

NORTH MALÉ
ATOLL

RASDHOO

SOUTH MALÉ
ATOLL

ARI
ATOLL

FELIDHU
ATOLL

FAAF
ATOLL

VATTARU

DHAAL
ATOLL

MEEMU
ATOLL

THAA
ATOLL

LAAMU
ATOLL

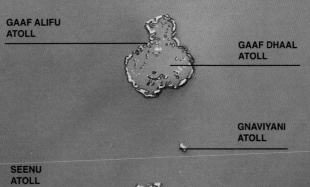

GAAF ALIFU
ATOLL

GAAF DHAAL
ATOLL

GNAVIYANI
ATOLL

SEENU
ATOLL

N

INTRODUCTION

The current must be kept in mind during all dives in the Maldives. Wherever you dive, either in the oceanic passes or the shoals within the atolls, the first thing to check before entering the water is the strength and direction of the current. The success of the dive almost always depends on these two variables. The Maldivian archipelago is swept by ceaseless currents which are caused by seasonal monsoons. Thus, the current will be running east to west when the winter winds blow from the northeast, with oceanic surface waters moving from west to east during the summer southwest monsoons. During certain periods of the day the movements of the sea increase the strength of the current, especially within the oceanic passes. One of the many advantages of a scuba diving cruise is that it is possible to dive during the best times of day in terms of light and currents.

Life on board revolves entirely around the needs of the scuba divers, without neglecting those passengers who are not divers, who will have the tender at their disposal to get off at the islands or go snorkeling on the reef.

Generally speaking, scuba divers frequent two types of areas, the passes - called *kandu* in Maldivian - and the emerging reefs within the atolls - *thilas* and *giris*. For safety reasons, but also because of the clearer water and greater variety of pelagic fish near the pass drop-offs, dives in oceanic channels should always be made with a moderate inflowing current. The dive should begin on the oceanic wall outside the atoll, about 50 meters away from the corner of the *kandu*. As the divers descend, the current carries them to the mouth of the channel, and after stopping at the drop-off, they enter the channel, being careful to stay as close as possible to one of the two inside walls of the pass when they come back up. Within the atolls are the *thilas*, shoals with a round or slightly elongated shape, which rise from a depth of about 35-40 meters to 5-15 meters from the surface and are usually swept by strong currents. The *giris*, which have more or less the same characteristics as the *thilas*, rise from a lesser depth, about 25-30 meters, and come nearly to the surface, never more than one meter below. Dives in these areas always begin from a certain distance from the coral formation, so that divers can descend to the desired depth regardless of the strength of the current. *Thilas* and *giris* always have a lee side where, sheltered from the current, you can ascend to shallow depths.

An underwater computer is strongly recommended in order to optimize the length of the dive in complete safety, using the multilevel system. A safety stop of at least 3 minutes at a depth of 4-5 meters is always necessary at the end of each dive. Another very useful accessory is a buoy, which can be sent to the surface while you make the safety stop at a depth of 5 meters. The buoy will emerge vertically from the water at a height of about one meter, thus permitting the *dhoni* crew to check the movements and position of the diving group. Water temperature is constant year round at about 26°-28° C, and thus a 3mm neoprene wetsuit will be all that you'll need.

A

B

C

D

A - A fleet of fishing dhonis *waiting to take to sea. This is in the Eydhafushi lagoon in the Baa Atoll.*

B - Natural marvels such as this are the order of the day when sailing the Maldivian islands.

C - The approach to the island of Ihuru is almost like coming to paradise on earth.

D - The Fathuhul Bari, *a cruise boat based on the design of a 19th century brig, rocks lazily in the wake of a* faru, *emerging reef.*

E - This aerial image makes it easy to distinguish the external portion of the reef, which plunges into the blue sea off the oceanic wall, from the internal portion.

CHOICE OF BOAT

F - A diving dhoni waits, following the bubbles that divers produce at the end of their dive. This system, known as drift-dive, is extremely safe.

E

F

G

H

G - An island has formed on the outside wall of the atoll; usually Maldivian land areas are agglomerates of sand and calcareous parts accumulated by the waves and held together by vegetation.

H - The outside edges of the atolls are frequently interrupted by deep channels, known as passes, through which water is exchanged between the internal lagoons and the ocean.

There are currently about 50 cruise boats in the Maldives, but not all of them offer good facilities. When choosing a boat, carefully evaluate its characteristics in order to avoid having your vacation in paradise turn into a week in hell. First of all, use a tour operator who is thoroughly experienced in charters, especially in the Maldives. The operator should have a fleet of boats sufficient to meet every need, from those of small groups of 4 to 6 friends to more spacious boats for groups of 10 to 12 persons. The operator should have an office in Malé and a warehouse with all equipment, including spare parts, needed to handle any emergency, especially compressors, the lifeblood of all scuba diving cruises. At present, *Seafari Adventure Club* of Monza, which markets its boats in Italy, France and Germany and has a decade of experience in the Maldives, can satisfy all these needs. In fact, it was even selected by American tour operators as a point of reference for cruises through the atolls, and anyone who knows the American tourism market knows how difficult it is to gain their trust! When you choose a boat, check to see that the number of bathrooms is adequate for the number of cabins. It is best if each cabin has a private bath. The cabins should have "European" size beds and be well ventilated. Some boats, such as the *Koimala* and the *Madivaru 3*, even have individual air conditioning systems. Common areas such as the dining room and the sun deck must be spacious enough for the number of guests on board, and electrical generators should have silencers and function long enough to recharge flashes and lighting equipment. The boat should have a reserve of fresh water for at least a seven day cruise. In any event, all Maldivian villages offer excellent fresh water to replenish reserves. The cook on board should be confident with the "international cuisine," as not everyone enjoys the strong spices of Oriental cooking, and a nice plate of spaghetti always puts cruise passengers in a good mood. The guide who accompanies passengers both on the cruise and underwater must have years of diving experience in the Maldives, be thoroughly familiar with the diving areas throughout the atolls and have good knowledge of marine biology to supplement the briefing with information on the environment and habits of fish. Life on board follows the rhythms of the sun: what with diving, snorkeling, visits to Maldivian villages and walks on desert islands, there will certainly be no time to get bored, and the days will pass pleasantly. Confirmed scuba divers will be in the water constantly, while those who love to relax will be lying lazily on the bridge, perhaps reading a good book. You don't need to pack much apart from personal scuba diving gear: T-shirts, shorts, wraparound skirts and swimming suits are everyday wear suitable for more "mundane" occasions such as visits to tourist resorts as well. Avoid rigid suitcases which are difficult to stow. In addition to the boat/hotel, there is the "diving dhoni", indispensable for the perfect management of dives and land excursions. *Dhonis*, characteristic Maldivian fishing boats, hold air tanks, all diving gear and compressors, so that the noise of generators does not disturb the guests. It is extremely convenient to leave your equipment in the roomy baskets, always ready for use, rather than struggling to carry it back after each dive. The only things which are usually brought back onto the boat are photography and video equipment, so that batteries may be recharged, lenses changed and rolls of film and cassettes replaced. This increases security, and each dive turns into a pleasant and relaxing drift dive, always with the current in favor.

UNDERWATER PHOTOGRAPHY

I t has for good reason been said that the Maldives are the best place in the world to photograph fish, as perhaps nowhere else is there such a variety of forms of life, corals and fish as in the Maldivian reefs. The only other place I have seen this much color and life is in the Egyptian Red Sea at the very end of the Sinai peninsula near Sharm El Sheikh, in the Ras Mohammed underwater park. Diving in the waters of the Maldives, it becomes relatively easy to approach any type of fish, depending on the type of seabed. In order to encounter and photograph large pelagic fish such as sharks, tunas, eagle rays and jacks, you should dive in the passes on the outside drop-off. In these cases it is advisable to reduce photography equipment to a minimum, keeping everything together so that you always have one hand free. Sometimes the current near the oceanic channels is very violent, and it becomes necessary to grab on to something in order to remain still. Optical systems that produce the best results on these occasions are the 28 mm and the 35 mm. If you are able to get very close to the subject, you can also use a 20 mm, but you will need to control your movements very carefully, as well as the noise caused by the exhalation bubbles that issue from the distributor. In order to get good images of the schools of fish that swim near the reef, as well as panoramic photos that catch a good portion of the reef and its inhabitants, you should dive on the shoals within the atolls. Under these circumstances you can calmly and carefully frame the best shot. The most suitable lenses are certainly wide-angle lenses such as the 15 mm *Nikonos* or the 14 mm or 18 mm mounted on a reflex in an underwater case. At present there are two photography systems, so to speak, that make it possible to obtain excellent results even if you are trying underwater photography for the first time. The most commonly used is the *Nikonos* amphibious system. Since the appearance of *Calypso*, the first underwater

C

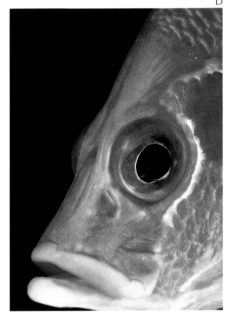

D

A

B

A - A large school of barracudas (Sphyraena qenie) *hovers under the keel of the boat. These swift predators are usually found in dense groups; only the largest individuals are solitary.*

B - *The silhouettes of a cruise boat and a support diving dhoni stand out on the surface over a seabed richly covered with soft and colorful alcyonarians.*

C - A diver *approaches a pair of bright red goggle eyes* (Priacanthus hamrur). *Usually these fish live in small groups on the inner shoals of the atolls.*

D - A good close-up of a saber squirrelfish (Sargocentron spiniferum). *This curious inhabitant of the reef usually lives sheltered in deep cracks with other individuals of the same species.*

system, it has developed the *Nikonos V*, with interchangeable lenses from 80 mm to 15 mm, and the *Nikonos RS* system, which includes an amphibious camera with a reflex vision and lenses from a 13 mm super wide-angle to a 50 macro autofocus. The second possibility in underwater photography is to use a normal land camera which has been protected in a special amphibious case, which makes it possible to use all the electronic functions of the camera and a wide range of lenses to meet every need. Macro photography deserves a separate discussion - corals of every size and shape are inhabited

G

E

H

F

I

E - A large humpback wrasse (Cheilinus undulatus) confidently approaches a group of divers; these Labridae *can reach up to 2 meters in length and weigh up to 200 kilos.*

F - A small goby (Bryaninops youngei) on a whip coral (Cirrhipathes anguina); due to its small size, about 3 centimetres, you need to keep a sharp eye in order to spot one as it moves jerkily along its branch of coral.

G - Meeting a dolphin in the open sea during a dive is a magical experience which is hard to forget!

H - Breathtaking encounters are possible in deeper water, in this case with a hammerhead shark (Sphyrna lewini), which advances gracefully with continuous movements of its long tail. It is very difficult to approach these pelagians, as they are disturbed by the noise of bubbles caused by divers.

A - An underwater video being shot of a group of bluestriped snappers (Lutjanus kasmira) *as they move in a compact school. This yellow mass in movement creates pleasant effects when filmed.*

by a myriad of little animals which sometimes escape a superficial view. These subjects are often no more than a centimeter long, but have incredible colors. The little shrimp in the sea anemones, the camouflaged crabs in the alcyonarians, the gobies in the sea fans and the crustaceans in the crinoids are just a few examples. In order to snap these "miniatures," depending on the photography system used, you will need additional lenses and extension tubes or micro lenses

C

A

D

B

in an underwater case.

With respect to lighting, in macro photography it is advisable to use two flashes so that there are no shadows in the photo. When the subjects have normal reflecting power, you can use TTL mode, which will give you automatically controlled exposure. With regard to films, when light is optimal you should use low sensitivity emulsions like the *64 ASA Kodachrome* or the *100 ASA Fuji.* For close-up photos use film no more sensitive than 50 ASA, which will perfectly reproduce all details. When you use photo equipment in salt water, you must thoroughly rinse all your equipment after each dive, if possible leaving it in fresh water for a few minutes. Afterwards, you should spray an anti-saline liquid such as *Salt-X* over all parts in order to eliminate the last traces of salt crystals. By doing this, you will lengthen the life of all your equipment. You should check all accessible O-rings at least once a day, carefully cleaning the seating and

B - Between one dive and another, photographers and video operators exchange advice and thoughts as they set up their equipment. A cruise is also a way to broaden one's knowledge and compare experiences.

C - A photographer frames a group of saber squirrelfish (Sargocentron spiniferum) *peering out from the entry of a grotto covered with colorful alcyonarians.*

D - A masked bannerfish (Heniochus monoceros) *poses for the photographer with the ease of a model. This is a rather rare shot, as this fish is considered one of the most timid inhabitants of the reef.*

E - An evening dive always holds pleasant surprises; even a reef which seems uninteresting by day will be full of brightly colored subjects at night, such as this fragile starfish (Ophiothrix purpurea) climbing up the expanded polyps of a sea-fan.

gently lubricating them to keep them soft and elastic. At least once a year you should have your camera checked by a specialized laboratory, which can examine all the functions out of your reach. Underwater photography is a goal for all divers who are looking for new ways to enrich their knowledge of scuba diving, and those who take underwater photos must therefore have good position control techniques in order to avoid damaging the reef. It is far too easy to forget the fragility of the corals when you are concentrating on framing a shot. Apart from film, all other photography equipment is impossible to find on the Maldives, so you should bring extra O-rings and all those little spare parts that can be invaluable in emergency situations. One final word of advice: don't try to learn underwater photography from those who are self-taught. Take a course instead, and you will avoid wasting rolls of film and becoming discouraged by the first disappointing results. Training in this area has truly progressed, with textbooks which are easy to understand and simple to apply. One of the best courses of this type is the specialized Underwater Photography Course taught by SSI, an American scuba diving training agency with branches in Europe and the rest of the world, which uses teaching systems translated in all languages.

F - Large sea-fans rise up from the bottom of the pass. The image is made more evocative by the diver in the background who, keeping perfectly still, holds a servo-flash in his hand.

G - At the entrance to the grottos, divers are often literally enveloped by clouds of glassfish (Parapriacanthus ransonneti). These little inhabitants of the cavities of the reef reflect the spotlights with golden flashes.

NORTH CRUISE ITINERARY

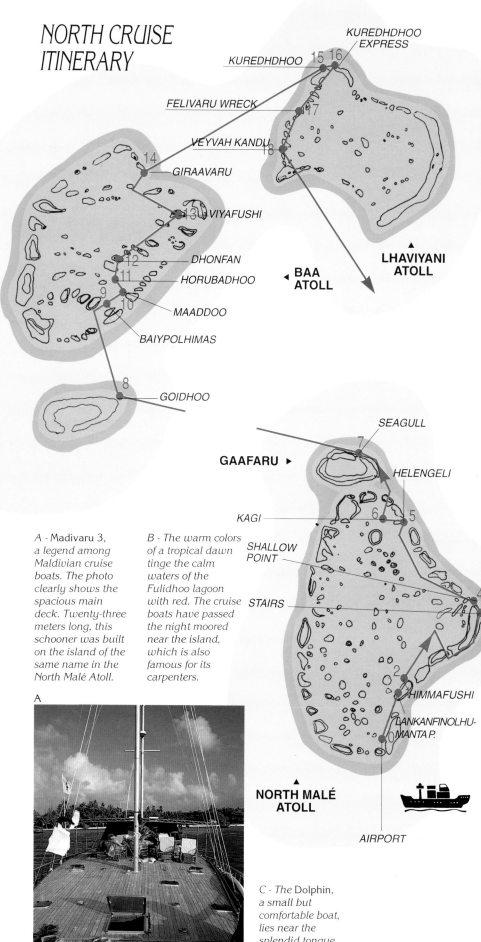

KUREDHDHOO
EXPRESS

KUREDHDHOO 15 16

FELIVARU WRECK 17

VEYVAH KANDU 18

14

GIRAAVARU

13 VIYAFUSHI

12 DHONFAN

11 HORUBADHOO

9

10

MAADDOO

BAIYPOLHIMAS

8 GOIDHOO

◄ BAA ATOLL

▲ LHAVIYANI ATOLL

SEAGULL 7

GAAFARU ►

HELENGELI

KAGI 6 5

SHALLOW POINT

STAIRS 4

2

HIMMAFUSHI

LANKANFINOLHU-MANTA P.

▲ NORTH MALÉ ATOLL

AIRPORT

A - Madivaru 3, a legend among Maldivian cruise boats. The photo clearly shows the spacious main deck. Twenty-three meters long, this schooner was built on the island of the same name in the North Malé Atoll.

B - The warm colors of a tropical dawn tinge the calm waters of the Fulidhoo lagoon with red. The cruise boats have passed the night moored near the island, which is also famous for its carpenters.

A

C - The Dolphin, a small but comfortable boat, lies near the splendid tongue of Foththeyo: this is one of the best moments to appreciate a boat holiday.

A scuba diving cruise in a well-equipped boat makes it possible to explore little-known areas, in particular the portions of the archipelago where tourism is still rare. For this reason, one of the most beautiful cruises is the one through the atolls north of Malé: Gaafaru-Goidhoo-Baa and Lhaviyani.

This new adventure begins from the lagoon of Farukolufushi, the Club Med lagoon where the boat moors while awaiting passengers, and heads north.

After assembling the equipment, pairing off and listening to a short briefing, everything is ready for the first dive at Lankanfinolhu or Manta Point, an easy dive to settle you in, that can nevertheless get your adrenaline going if you see the school of young mantas that has made this diving area famous.

We'll moor for the night in the lagoon of Himmafushi, where you can go to the nearby resort to make telephone calls. Our first wake-up on the boat is fantastic: the absolute peace that surrounds us truly makes it feel as if we were at the ends of the earth.

The first dive of the day is outside the Thulusdhoo Pass, on the oceanic wall at a point called Stairs, a true paradise for photographers given the great concentration of marine life, including sweetlips, snappers, whitetip sharks and eagle rays. This area even has one of the few points where leopard sharks can be glimpsed: Shallow Point, where you can make your second dive of the day. Heading north, we find one of the most beautiful *thilas* for diving, Helengeli, where a truly thrilling dive is possible. Before leaving the Atoll of Kaafu, we can relax for an afternoon, going snorkeling or lazily sunning in the sand, waiting for the night dive on the *giri* of the desert island at Kagi. Continuing our cruise, we leave "tourist civilization" behind. From now on we'll see only two tourist villages, and we'll have an opportunity to observe the true customs and lifestyles of the Maldivian people. In Gaafaru, an enormous coral

D - The pass is the great door that leads out to the open sea. The depth of the channels varies from thirty to forty meters, while their length may range from a few dozen meters to several kilometers.

E - A dhoni approaches the emerging reef that surrounds the desert island of Aarah (Felidu Atoll). It is almost always possible for the boat to anchor right on the beach so that passengers may take a walk.

ring with a single island of Maldivian fishermen, famous for its many shipwrecks, we'll dive around the most interesting one, the *Seagull.* This is an exciting dive, both due to the wreck and to the marine life we may encounter: large tunas, jacks and gray sharks. Those who enjoy troll fishing can indulge in this sport by crossing the arm of ocean between Gaafaru and Goidhoo on one of the *dhonis,* as this is one of the best fishing areas in the archipelago. Goidhoo, where there are four islands of fishermen, is one of the most beautiful atolls of the Maldives. The diving area, Goidhoo Outside, is so beautiful that you'll want to make repeated dives. The red coral (and it goes without saying that it is absolutely forbidden to pick any of it) and

B

C

D

E

the crystal clear water make this place truly unique.
In the evening, seated on the bridge of the boat waiting for sunset, you may see dolphins playfully leaping as they bid farewell to another exciting day. The crossing from Goidhoo to Baa is brief. The Baa Atoll has only one tourist village, Soneva Fushi, on the island of Kunfunadhoo, opened in 1995.
For those who love the life of Robinson Crusoe, this atoll is truly an earthly paradise.
You can peacefully loaf on the sunny beaches, explore the

interior of the islands, full of coconut palms, and with a bit of luck watch the sea turtles deposit their eggs at sunset. The most beautiful dives at Baa are on the numerous shoals within the atoll: Maaddoo Giri, Horubadhoo Thila, Dhonfan Thila and Baiypolhi Mas. In these areas, where scuba divers are rare and the seabeds are intact, there is a true explosion of underwater life. The walls, full of nooks and crannies, are completely covered with alcyonarians and sea fans, among which swim thousands of reef fish. The ceaseless currents carry in food for the large pelagic fish, so that you may see barracudas, jacks, gray sharks,

nurse sharks and shovel-nosed rays. A particularly exciting dive is among the thousands of batfish that populate the giri of Baiypolhi Mas. During this dive you are completely surrounded by batfish swimming peacefully around you. The boat moors for the night near Viyafushi, a desert island and a pearl of the Maldivian sea. While we walk along the white sand beach that fringes the island and watch evening approach, the crew is preparing a barbecue of freshly caught fish by the light of a bonfire. Thus ends another thrilling day on the sea. When we leave the Atoll of Baa we enter the Lhaviani Atoll, and the boat heads toward Kuredhdhoo, the only tourist island on the atoll, with the largest village in the Maldives. This is almost a mandatory stop after so much close contact with nature, and we change our pace here for an evening and enjoy a good beer. The first dive is in the Fehigili Pass, known as Kuredhdhoo Express, where you can explore the numerous grottos carpeted with lilac and pale blue alcyonarians or else stay at the base of the pinnacle, looking off into the blue depths to glimpse gray sharks, tunas, eagle rays and entire families of humphead wrasses. On our way back south we'll dive at the wrecks at

Felivaru, a large island where a factory that produces canned tuna is located. Due to the richness of these waters, the two wrecks of Japanese cargo ships are totally covered with alcyonarians, and batfish, emperors, groupers and millions of glassfish swim about. Photography fans will find this a true garden of Eden.
Before returning to the North Malé Atoll, we make the long crossing of one of the largest oceanic channels, Kashidhoo Channel. We thus come to the end of our cruise in the North Malé Atoll, where we finish off with a beautiful dive at Paradise Rocks.

The name itself gives you an idea of what you can expect in this area: sea turtles, oriental sweetlips, snappers and clouds of anthias. The boat returns to the Club Med lagoon, where you can organize a visit to the tourist village or some last minute shopping in Malé.

A - This hawkfish (Paracirrhites forsteri) is lying among the corals, hoping for some prey to pass within attacking range.

B - A photographer cautiously

approaches a turtle (Caretta caretta). These prehistoric-looking creatures today are protected with a program approved by the Malé government that prohibits their sale and capture.

C - These flower-like organisms are in reality tube-shaped worms that wave their plumed corollas in order to capture the plankton on which they feed.

D - A large sea fan stretches upwards. At its base a white-bellied damselfish defends its territory by attacking anyone who approaches.

E - The form of a diver is silhouetted against the sun, with large sea-fans in the foreground.

These horny corals always grow perpendicular to the direction of the prevailing currents.

F - Yellowtail fairy basslets (Pseudanthias evansi) photographed against the light near the upper portion of the reef.

G - This firegoby (Nemateleotris decora) can often be observed while hovering within a half meter of the bottom, facing to the current to feed on plankton.

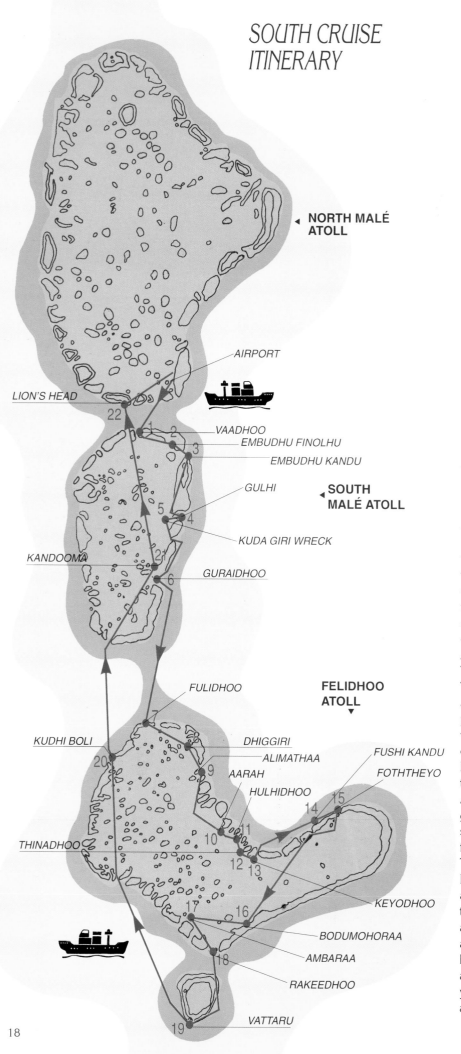

SOUTH CRUISE ITINERARY

NORTH MALÉ ATOLL ◄

AIRPORT

LION'S HEAD
22

1   2   VAADHOO
        EMBUDHU FINOLHU
    3   EMBUDHU KANDU

GULHI   ► **SOUTH MALÉ ATOLL**

5
    4

KUDA GIRI WRECK

KANDOOMA
        21
    6   GURAIDHOO

FULIDHOO   **FELIDHOO ATOLL** ▼

7

KUDHI BOLI   DHIGGIRI
20   ALIMATHAA
        9   AARAH   FUSHI KANDU
            HULHIDHOO   FOTHTHEYO
                    14 15
            11
THINADHOO   10
        12 13

                    KEYODHOO
        17 16
                BODUMOHORAA
            18 AMBARAA
        RAKEEDHOO

19   VATTARU

18

The cruise described below is usually 10 to 14 days long, depending on how much time cruise passengers want to spend in each area. The ship always sails in the calm waters within the atolls, except for one hour as it crosses the channel between South Malé and Felidu. Normally passengers sleep in the immediate vicinity of the next day's dive. Getting from one point to another requires a maximum of two hours of sailing, usually during the middle of the day. This itinerary includes the Atolls of South Malé, where there are still tourist villages, as well as the Felidu Atoll, with its splendid deserted islands and the famous dives in the passes, where encounters with pelagic fish are possible. Depending on weather conditions and supply needs, the cruise boats are usually moored and waiting for passengers in the lagoon of Farukolufushi or in the port of Malé. *Dhonis* are used for the short trip from the international airport at Hulule to embarkation points. After quickly settling into our cabins and being quickly briefed about life on board, we're off! Manoeuvering through the numerous cargo ships at the end of Malé harbor, the ship exits from the Hulule Pass and heads south, and crossing the Malé channel enters the atoll of South Malé through the Vaadhoo Pass. The first dive is at Vaadhoo Caves. This is an easy dive among a myriad of reef fish that live protected in the cavities of the walls. At night we moor in the calm lagoon of Emboodhu Finolhu, where you can get off at the resort to make telephone calls. As the new day dawns and you gaze at the spectacular natural setting around you, you'll truly feel like you're in another world. The first dive of the day is at Emboodhu Kandu, where, allowing yourself to be carried by the current, you'll pass eagle rays and sharks. Heading south, we arrive at Gulhi, an island inhabited by Maldivians where there is a shipyard. With a bit of luck, you may see a launching, where all the inhabitants of the village

A - The photo shows the oceanic front where the waves break. During dives in these areas, which drop off vertically into the blue depths, any kind of encounter is possible.

help hoist the boat onto tree trunks and drag it into the water. Here it is possible to explore the *Kuda Giri Wreck*, the remains of a small cargo ship populated by groupers and batfish. In this area breathtaking encounters with the gray sharks of the Gulhi Pass are possible. Moving into the central part of the atoll, we pass the islands of Biyaadhoo and Vilivaru, recognizable from the thick coconut palm plantations that surround the tourist villages. Then we come to Guraidhoo, a large Maldivian fishing island

C

A

D

B

where even the most hardened shoppers will be pleasantly impressed by the large quantity of souvenirs that the numerous shops offer. At sunset at the end of the day, stretched out on the bridge of the boat in complete relaxation, you can see hundreds of dolphins heading out to the open sea. This mooring spot also offers the opportunity for a pleasant evening dive. One of the most thrilling underwater experiences of the Maldives is possible in this island pass - Guraidhoo Corner, where there are large sharks, entire families of humphead wrasses, barracudas, jacks and tunas. The voyage goes on to Felidu, one of the most beautiful atolls in the Maldives, where there are only two tourist villages and some of the most lovely desert islands in the entire archipelago. The voyage is always accompanied by the playful leaps of the dolphins. Sportsmen can make the crossing aboard the

B - Shipwrecks are true oases where one can observe an extremely high concentration of life forms within a very limited space. Alcyonarians and hard corals have grown on the beams of this ship.

C - Cruise boats always sail calm waters. A vacation among the Maldivian atolls is thus recommended even for non-divers.

D - This species of bannerfish (Heniochus monoceros) sometimes forms dense schools near the seabed, but never at depths of over 30 meters.

A - A crinoid distends its numerous arms in order to capture plankton. Usually these starfish are nocturnal, but in areas where the currents are strong they are active during the day as well.

diving *dhoni*, where they can go troll fishing. King fish, tuna and sailfish offer exciting combat. The first island we come to is Fulidhoo, where we make our first contacts with true Maldivian civilization. The island is the launching point for two extraordinary dives, Dhiggiri Corner and Miaru Kandu, where in the garden of the pass you may meet anything from hammerheads to gray sharks, eagle rays and giant tunas, and where a truly rare species exists - the small yellow and violet blue ribbon eel. Moving along the east side of the atoll, you can dive into the lagoon of a true pearl of the Maldivian archipelago: the little island of Aarah, a desert island fringed with white sand beaches and covered with thick vegetation crowned by tall coconut palms. You can go snorkeling in the blue waters of the lagoon, among clouds of little fish. In the evening, after a long day of diving in the grottos of Hulhidhoo, an easy dive among the colorful alcyonarians that carpet the breaks and recesses in

B

C

A

the walls, and in the Thinadhoo Pass, where at the end of the dive you can see manta rays stopped at the "grooming station" in the channel, we'll go to the island of Keyodhoo to see a typical dance of Maldivian fishermen, the *Bodu Beru*. The rhythmic beat of the drums and the movements of the dancers create a magical atmosphere that takes you back through time.

At the most easterly point of the entire Maldivian archipelago you can dive into a true sanctuary, Foththeyo, which is considered to be one of the ten most beautiful dives in the world. The explosion of color and the quantity of soft corals literally leaves divers open-mouthed. Sometimes you may meet one of the local residents, a giant grouper over two meters long with a prehistoric appearance. This place is so beautiful that you'll want to make repeated dives. The boat will moor for the night near the tongue of white sand near the channel, where the full moon reflecting on the

B - A coral grouper (Cephalopholis miniata) *makes a sudden turn among the protuberances of the reef.*

C - A turtle (Eretmochelys imbricata) *peacefully swims close by the upper part of the reef. Turtles are primarily carnivorous. Their diet includes jelly-fish, crabs, cattle-fish and other small fish.*

F

D - Black-footed clownfish (Amphiprion nigripes) move timidly in the shelter of the sea anemone which protects them from dangerous predators. This species is common throughout the Maldives.

glittering white sand becomes a spectacular, unparalleled vision of beauty. Proceeding with the cruise, we arrive at Bodu Mohora, a desert island so beautiful that its owner charges people to get off there. You will truly feel like Robinson Crusoe here, walking on the white, deserted beach and venturing inland to gather a few coconuts. In the evening, by the light of a bonfire on the deserted beach of Ambaraa, the crew will prepare a barbecue of freshly-caught fish. Thus ends another magical day in intimate contact with the sea. In this area you'll also be able to dive in Rakeedhoo Pass, with its terraces of violet alcyonarians and schools of jacks and numerous groupers. Passing whales have often been sighted in the channel between Rakeedhoo and the nearby atoll of Vattaru. The first stop on the return trip north is Kudhi Boli, where you can dive on a shoal with a top reef 5 meters from the surface, famous for its red-orange alcyonarians. It truly seems a dive

D

E

into an aquarium, given the huge numbers of reef fish such as parrotfish, anthias, butterflyfish and sea turtles. We return to the South Malé Atoll, and during our trip to the capital we'll dive at Kandooma Corner, where there are numerous stingrays drowsing on the bottom, as well as schools of fusiliers and butterflyfish.
The cruise ends with a flourish at the "shark circus" at Lion's Head. Here, on a natural terrace, you can watch shark feeding as numerous gray sharks, attracted by the food thrown into the water, swim around the divers. The boat returns to the tranquil lagoon of Club Med, where you can organize a visit to Malé for your final purchases of handicrafts and souvenirs, or else arrange a tour of the capital.

E - Stingrays (Taeniura melanospilos) are a frequent sight when diving in sandy areas or near horizontal cracks in the walls.

F - Oriental sweetlips (Plectorhinchus orientalis) are among the most photogenic and friendly fish. They live in groups and do not mind the presence of photographers.

ARI CRUISE ITINERARY

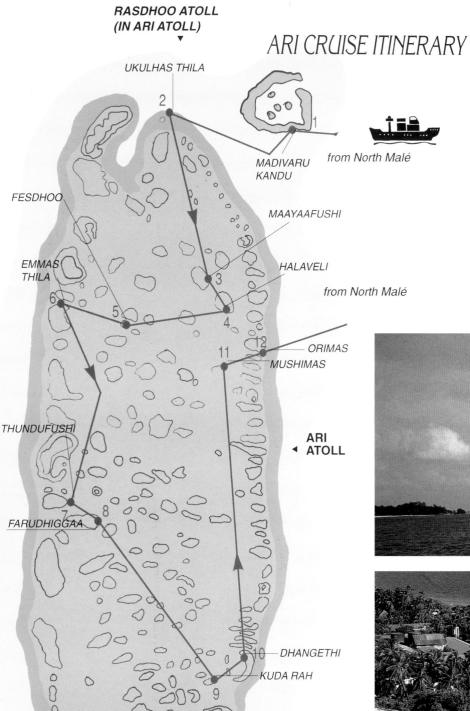

UKULHAS THILA

2

1

MADIVARU
KANDU

from North Malé

FESDHOO

MAAYAAFUSHI

3

HALAVELI

EMMAS
THILA

from North Malé

6

5

4

ORIMAS

11   12   MUSHIMAS

ARI
◄ ATOLL

THUNDUFUSHI

7   8

FARUDHIGGAA

10   DHANGETHI

KUDA RAH

9

One of the most beautiful cruises in the Maldivian archipelago is to the Ari Atoll, departing from the North Malé Atoll. Heading toward the western side of the North Malé Atoll, we reach the island of Rasfari, where we can make the first dives of our cruise. The first is at Okobe Thila, a very colorful dive due to the great numbers of alcyonarians and the thousands of butterflyfish and snappers that inhabit the area. We'll also dive at Rasfari Thila, which provides the first thrills of the cruise due to the large numbers of gray sharks. The crossing of the oceanic arm is interrupted by the

A - An artificial pass was dug in the reef that encloses this lagoon in order to permit boats to reach the village pier.

B - Some cruise boats also have sails which are hoisted during longer crossings when the winds are favorable.

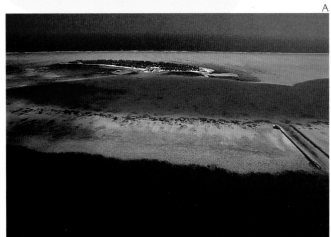

Rasdhoo Atoll, a must for one of the most beautiful dives anywhere in the Maldives - Madivaru Kandu, with its hammerhead sharks. We'll continue our crossing to reach Ari, but before entering the atoll we'll dive on the Ukulhas Shoal, a grooming station for the mantas, where these "lords of the sea" are always present. We'll moor for the night in the lagoon of the island of Ukulhas, where we can visit the village of Maldivian fishermen as we wait for dinner. The dives planned for the next day cause a great deal of excitement. First there is Maya Thila, where you'll find all the gray sharks you ever wanted to see. This is a constantly thrilling dive, with sharks everywhere, and when you decide to surface, you'll be accompanied by a gray shark almost to the *dhoni*. The second dive is no less exciting, as you'll have the chance to explore the wreck of Halaveli, where stingrays are permanent residents that will play with the divers. In the evening the boat moors in the lagoon of Halaveli, and you'll be able to go to the tourist resort to get an ice cream or make a telephone call. Our voyage continues as we head west to dive near the *Fesdhoo Wreck*, an easy but very colorful dive, as the wreckage of the ship has been encrusted with brightly colored colonies of coral polyps. Photography fans will find this a true paradise of colors.

After spending the night moored near the island of Fesdhoo, where there is a tourist village, we'll move to the western side of the atoll for two dives that provide some unique sensations - Emmas Thila and Panettone. The high concentration of plankton carried in by the current makes these two areas the best points for viewing mantas.

In addition, the walls of the *thila* are covered with soft coral, among which swim clouds of anthias, bannerfish and, given the exposure to currents, pelagic fish such as barracudas, jacks and sharks. This thrilling day will come to a perfect close with a jaunt to the discotheque in the tourist village on the island of Thundufushi. Our ocean voyage wouldn't be complete without a stop at Farudhigga, a stupendous little desert island that seems suspended on the Maldivian Sea, where we can relax on the shining white sand and enjoy a romantic evening barbecue on the beach, with freshly caught fish prepared by crew members. It's a real cure-all after so much of the "mundane" world. We'll come to the far south of the Ari Atoll, where we'll dive at Kudarah Thila, an area extremely rich with marine life due to the

D

E

ever-present currents that carry in nourishment for large tunas, schools of jacks, humphead wrasses and eagle rays. Before heading back north, we'll stop in Dhangethi, a large island of fishermen, where the very low prices make shopping nearly a must. On our return we'll stop at one of the temples of scuba divers - Shark Thila, made famous by the large number of gray sharks. These unpredictable inhabitants of the sea are always present, and the area is so thrilling that you will want to make one dive after another.

But unfortunately we have to return, and we'll dive one last time at Orimas Thila, where it's almost always possible to see a feathertail stingray, as well as a myriad of brightly colored reef fish. The boat will moor in the Farukolufushi lagoon waiting for departure.

C - A brilliant white beach encircles this island where Kuda Rah, a tourist village, is located. There are about seventy international resorts on the Maldives, ranging from rather Spartan lodgings to luxury accommodations.

D - A vigorous forest of sea fans has grown on a protuberance on the outside wall of the atoll, due to the current which constantly brings in nourishment.

E - Two elegant examples of gray sharks (Carcharhinus amblyrhynchos) patrols the summit of a thila. A school of batfish hovers in the open water, their snouts to the current.

NORTH MALÉ ATOLL

The Kaafu Atoll includes the two old northern and southern atolls of Malé, the political and economic center of the country. Of this long chain of islands, which stretches out for 80 miles from north to south, only ten are inhabited by indigenous peoples.

On most of other islands, tourist villages have been developed. The local population has become involved in new tourism related industries such as the making and selling of souvenirs and local handicraft.

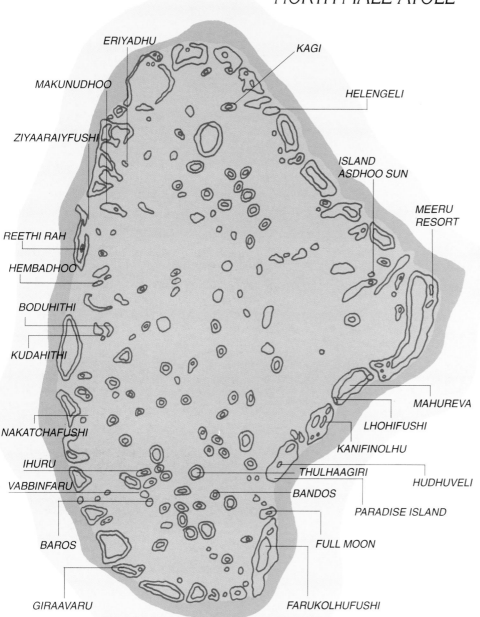

ERIYADHU
KAGI
MAKUNUDHOO
HELENGELI
ZIYAARAIYFUSHI
ISLAND ASDHOO SUN
MEERU RESORT
REETHI RAH
HEMBADHOO
BODUHITHI
KUDAHITHI
NAKATCHAFUSHI
MAHUREVA
IHURU
LHOHIFUSHI
VABBINFARU
KANIFINOLHU
THULHAAGIRI
HUDHUVELI
BANDOS
PARADISE ISLAND
BAROS
FULL MOON
GIRAAVARU
FARUKOLHUFUSHI

A

B

A - Similar to precious green emerald the Maldivian atolls characterize the dark blue of the Indian Ocean.

B - A sailing dhoni is getting close to the island of Vabbinfaru.

C - The vivid color of the undewater are one of the main charcateristics of the whole archipelago of the Maldives.

D - In this photograph can be observed the well known village of

Full Moon on the Island of Furanafushi.

E - This aereal view let you admire some of the main features of the Maldives: atolls, passes, and sand banks, their shape depending on the waves system and on currents.

F - This group of surgeonfish (Acanthurus mata) includes individuals of the same species but with different colors. They swim near the vertical walls and feed on zooplankton.

SOME RESORTS IN
NORTH MALÉ ATOLL

Kurumba, the first resort opened in the Maldives, in October 1972, is still very popular, not only because it is quite near the airport, but also because it has constantly renovated over the years, maintaining its own style. Today it is a grand hotel island with 190 rooms, some cottage style, and several suites, all with private gardens on the beach, a sports center with a sauna and jacuzzi, swimming pool and billiards room.

On the south side of the atoll is **Giraavaru**, one of the smaller resorts. Its 48 rooms are in two floor blocks on the lovely beach, and the island has a soft and

romantic atmosphere.

Baros, an hour by *dhoni* from the airport, has been open since 1973 and is especially popular with the English. It was recently renovated, with several octagonal-shaped wooden cottages constructed on piles. In the middle of the atoll is **Vabbinfaru**, opened in 1977 and rebuilt in 1995. It is now called Banyan Tree. Has 48 rooms. Large sandy and clear lagoon.

Ihuru has 44 well-furnished rooms along the splendid beach. The village was completely rebuilt in 1989, with comfortable basic finishing touches. The food is excellent. Intimate and informal

A - A classic image of Ihuru, an island paradise: the colorful sail on the beach adds to the "vacation effect."

B - Two turists are relaxing on the white beach of the Mahureva resort, on the island of Gasfinolhu.

atmosphere. Winner of National award for the preservation and protection of the environment in 1996.

Nakatchafushi, or "flower island," renovated in 1995, has a cozy atmosphere, with its five-sided, thatch-roofed cottages and Chinese restaurant.

Kudahithi is a little islet with only 7 fancifully named bungalows, all with theme furnishings, such as the Sheikh's Room and the Captain's Cabin. This is a luxury village with high standards of service and privacy. It is the only Maldivian resort without a diving center.

Boduhithi, which also offers sports facilities at Kudahithi, which is under the same management (Club Vacanze), is a village with an emphasis on sports, with 90 rooms built in masonry, four of which are on the water, discreet entertainment and good food.

Hembadhoo, a small island with basic but comfortable structures with few luxuries, has a pier on

C

D

A

B

both sides of the island. Its chalet-style living units are popular with German and Swiss visitors.

Reethi Rah is on the western side of the atoll. All its bungalows face the inner lagoon on a beautiful beach. The island's vegetation has intentionally been allowed to grow uncontrolled, giving it an overall wild appearance. Ten cottages are built on the water. It has an international clientele and a truly relaxing atmosphere.

Ziyaaraiyfushi resort is especially popular with Germans. It has simple yet functional structures, with sand floors in all common areas.

Makunudu: the resort was opened in 1983 and renovated in 1994. It has bungalows with verandahs on the beach. Cosy atmosphere, it has 31 rooms.

Eriyadhu, a lovely, oval-shaped island surrounded by a wide beach, has facilities overlooking a splendid lagoon. Friendly atmosphere and sense of relaxation. Central European clientele.

Helengeli closed for rebuilting,

C - The tourist resorts of Baros, that can be observed in this picture, is just an hour by dhoni from the airport of Malé.

D - A lagoon characterized by extremly cristalline water embraces the resort of Full Moon, just 30 minutes boat from the airport.

the resort opens in December 1996 with 50 rooms. It is quite popular with scuba divers due to its fortunate position on the north-east edge of the atoll.

Asdhoo Sun Island has 30 rooms in blocks of 2-3 rather rustic dwellings. Common areas are built very simply and have an Italian feel. It has a small beach.

Meeru Resort, on the island of Meerufenfushi, is one of the most crowded villages, with 214 rooms in blocks of 4-6 units. Nevertheless there is great respect for nature, an informal atmosphere and few concessions to luxury.

Mahureva, on the island of Gasfinolhu, is a functional village under Italian management (VALTUR), with an emphasis on sports. It has 40 masonry bungalows immersed in

E

vegetation, with a small "private beach," and a sense of privacy and freedom.

In 1975 the **Island of Lhohifushi** was used as an experimental plantation for coconut palms, then in 1979 the first tourist village was built there.
After being renovated in 1992, it now has 130 cabanas with coral walls in a thick forest of palms and fruit trees.

In 1978 the **Island of Kanifinolhu** had space for 18 visitors; now it has 300 beds with

carefully designed Maldivian-style dwellings hidden in luxuriant vegetation. The reception area and bar are in the form of traditional Maldivian boats. European and Australian clientele.

Hudhuveli has 44 rooms with an Italian atmosphere, catering to a primarily Italian clientele. Entertainment and club atmosphere.

Paradise Island is on the island of Lankanfinolhu, which was artificially elongated to two and a half times its original size to provide space for 100 rooms and 40 futuristically designed cottages. The living units stand in the middle of a botanical garden, with a nursery that contains many plant species, with various Japanese-style areas; numerous bars and restaurants are open 24 hours a day.

Thulhaagiri has a beautiful beach with 58 cabanas hidden among the bougainvillea, with a central European clientele.

Bandos, opened in 1972, with 220 beds, now has room for 650 visitors, and offers services that include a sports center, Thai massages, a convention hall and squash courts. On Friday it is frequented by many Europeans who reside in Malé.

Full Moon, on the Island of Furana, is about 30 minutes from the airport. Recently constructed, it has 53 lodges on the lagoon and nightly entertainment. Good service and facilities. It has 156 rooms.

Farukolhufushi, with its 152 room Club Med, has a splendid lagoon where one can often see cruise boats waiting for passengers, given the proximity of the airport.

F

G

H

E - At Ihuru it is possible directly from the bar terrace, admire the splendid lagoon around the island, and the sconfinate ocean.

F - A tourist enters in the warm waters of the lagoon of Giraavaru. The water temperature in the Maldives is between 26 and 30 degrees Centigrade year-round.

G, H - In these two areal shots can be observed completely and in particulat the resort of Kurumba. It is the first resort that opened in the Maldives. It is anyway very popular even today and not only because it is quite near the airport, but also because it has renovated over the years.

LION'S HEAD

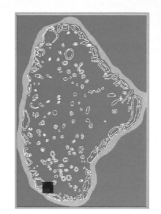

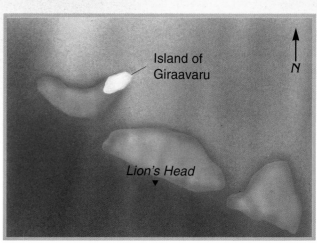

Island of
Giraavaru

Lion's Head

N

0 m

12 m

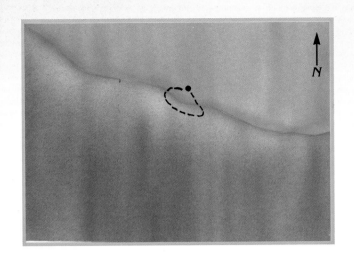

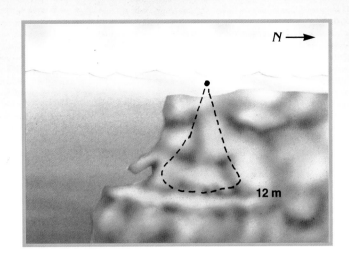

12 m

A - In the background a gray shark can be seen with its entourage of rainbow runners (Elagatis bipinnulata).
A pair of batfish (Platax teira) can also be seen.

B - Two large gray reef sharks have approached the photographer curiously.

C - The diver is nearly hidden by an imposing formation of sponges that grow by branching out upwards. Shy scalefin anthias (Pseudanthias squamipinnis) move among the tangled branches.

LOCATION

Lion's Head lies outside the South Malé Atoll, on the far southern edge. It is a part of the oceanic wall in the channel that separates the two Malé Atolls. At a depth of 12 meters is a cavern with a large overhanging coral spur to the west. The wall then continues vertically to the floor, occasionally broken by a few cracks.

DESCRIPTION OF THE DIVE

Apart from the beauty of the wall itself, Lion's Head is known for its gray sharks. There is a group of about twelve gray sharks in this area which are accustomed to being fed by certain very expert divemasters. Usually the divers stand with their backs to the wall, and the guide, bringing several small tunas into the water, stands before the group a few meters away. The most enterprising sharks immediately approach to snap at the fish and begin a frenetic swirl at close range. After about 10 minutes of this "show," you can proceed along the wall, ending the dive on the partially submerged reef.

C

A

D

B

In addition to the sharks, there are schools of dentex in this dive which, attracted by the lavish "booty," wait at the water's surface in anticipation of a mouthful. There are splendid formations of hard coral on the wall, especially shallow depths, and careful observers may encounter a few examples of stonefish. Turtles are also present, usually resting on the reef; as soon as approached they move away swiftly with powerful strokes of their flippers.
At a depth of 5-8 meters you may see dense schools of surgeonfish.

D - Near the surface of the reef it is not unusual to see sea turtles, in this case Eretmochelys imbricata, which rise to the surface to breathe.

30

E - Unfortunately, the number of sharks is seriously decreasing due to overfishing. If these selective predators disappear, the whole reef ecosystem is at risk.

F - Schools of yellowtail surgeonfish (Acanthurus xanthopterus) gather in dense groups near the reef.

At times these groups consist of hundreds of individuals that form an enormous white and blue mass. Given the position, and perhaps due to the excitement created by the shark feeding, you may be surprised by other large predators during this dive. Shark feeding is always potentially dangerous, and it is best to leave it to those with sufficient experience. If you want to watch one of these "shows," you should stay well against the wall and avoid moving until the sharks finish their meal and disappear into the blue depths.

G

E

F

H

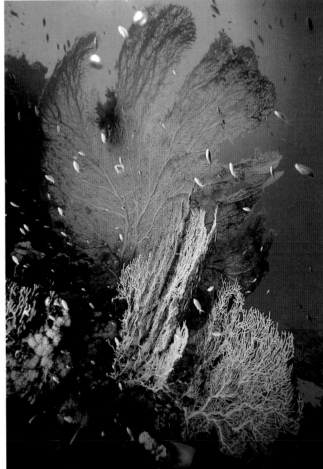

PHOTOGRAPHY

When visibility is good, excellent photos of sharks can be taken at Lion's Head. As the animals come quite close to the divers, in order to get a full frame shot at a distance of two meters you should use 20 to 24 millimeter lenses. For the large schools of snappers or surgeonfish, which are easy to approach, you can get excellent shots using a 15 millimeter wide-angle lens. Good close-up shots of fish are possible with 55 or 60 millimeter lenses.

G - Two large specimens of stonefish (Synanceia verrucosa), perfectly camouflaged on a detritic area of the reef. This is probably the most poisonous species of fish in the world.

H - The sun filters through the delicate fronds of sea-fans, producing beautiful plays of light.

HEMBADHOO WRECK

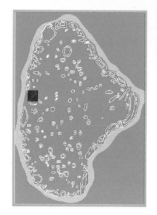

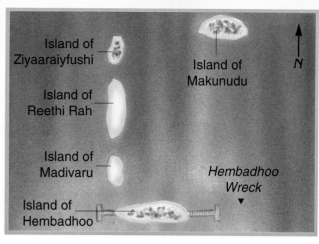

Island of Ziyaaraiyfushi

Island of Makunudu

Island of Reethi Rah

Island of Madivaru

Hembadhoo Wreck

Island of Hembadhoo

N

0 m

15 m

22 m

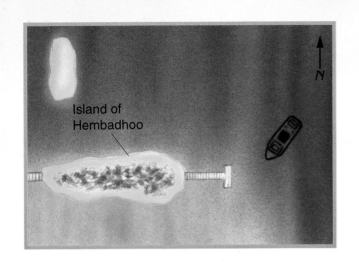

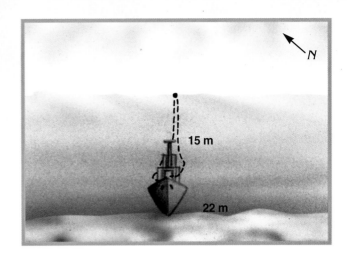

A - Diving onto
a sunken
shipwreck is
always a very
special experience;
be sure to follow
the directions of
the diving guide
in order to make
the most of the visit.

B - Numerous
species live
protected in the
thousands of
crevices formed
by the sunken hull,
like this pair of
red groupers
(Cephalopholis
miniata).

LOCATION

The wreck is situated in the northern part of the Malé Atoll, to be exact, on the eastern side of the resort island of Hembadhoo. The boat was specially sunk four years ago to create a point of attraction for scuba divers, and in short time became the pride of the diving school operated by Tashi. The cargo ship, about 18 meters long, is positioned in a north-south direction and lies on a seabed 22 meters deep. The first structures can be found at a depth of 15 meters.

DESCRIPTION OF THE DIVE

The exact point is marked by a buoy to which it is forbidden to moor, so the mooring line can be used for the descent and ascent. In this case the diving *dhoni* will move far from the area, waiting for the divers to surface. Another possibility is to have the divemaster enter the water first and descend to attach a line to the portions of the wreck which are not covered with corals.
In this manner, the support boat can wait in the area. Due to its shallow depth and the weak currents, this dive is appropriate for all levels of expertise.
A myriad of fish has found a new home in the metallic structures, and corals have also encrusted and covered the entire boat, creating a truly interesting oasis of life.
As soon as divers descend to the bridge of the wreck, the head of the house will come out to welcome them - a large humphead wrasse known as Bruno, who will follow them curiously throughout the entire dive. You will encounter numerous morays, some of which peep out of the portholes, while others are intent on being groomed by shrimp. Inside what was once the cabin, silvery clouds of glassfish move jerkily as a grouper passes. Eagle rays regularly frequent

D

A

B

C

E

C - A cleaner shrimp (Leandrites cyrtorhynchus) *intent on removing parasites from the skin of a moray* (Gymnothorax flavimarginatus). *These shrimps even enter the mouths of fish that submit to their care, removing bits of food trapped between their teeth.*

D - Usually it is not necessary to enter the structure unless there is something particular to see; simply examine the superstructures to discover all types of fish: in this case a humpback wrasse (Cheilinus undulatus).

E - An emperor angelfish (Pomacanthus imperator) has chosen the contorted wreck of the ship for its home.

F - A teardrop blenny (Ecsenius lineatus) takes refuge in a hole, perhaps frightened by the approach of a diver. These little animals reach no more than 8-10 centimeters in length.

G - A close-up of this grouper (Plectropomus areolatus) shows his impressive set of teeth. Curving inwards, these teeth serve to grasp prey.

the area, gliding elegantly near the surface, and large tunas also pass by, probably attracted by the schools of small fish that reside near the sunken cargo ship.

First of all, keep in mind that even though the wreck is inanimate, it has been transformed into a normal part of the coral reef and must be treated accordingly. Thus, it is important to keep your position under control in order to avoid damaging the corals that embellish the structure.

As the interior is rather cramped, it is better to stay outside.

It is very important not to feed the humphead wrasse, to avoid changing its feeding habits, giving it significant digestive problems and making it aggressive to divers. In addition, it should not be touched with gloves, as this may damage the protective mucus and encourage skin parasites.

PHOTOGRAPHY

As the wreck is small, you can use a fisheye lens to catch it all in a single photo. It is best to use natural lighting as much as possible, perhaps holding the flash up, mounted on a long arm to minimize shadows. The humphead wrasse, who is not at all afraid of divers, will certainly show up for photographs. Using macro lenses, the little shrimp in the mouths of the morays are quite "photogenic."

H - An eagle ray (Aetobatus narinari) appears from the blue depths and glides toward the seabed.

I - The silvery scales of these jacks illuminates the watery depths.

BLUE CANYON

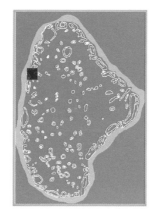

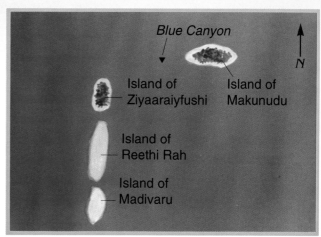

Blue Canyon

Island of Ziyaaraiyfushi

Island of Makunudu

Island of Reethi Rah

Island of Madivaru

N

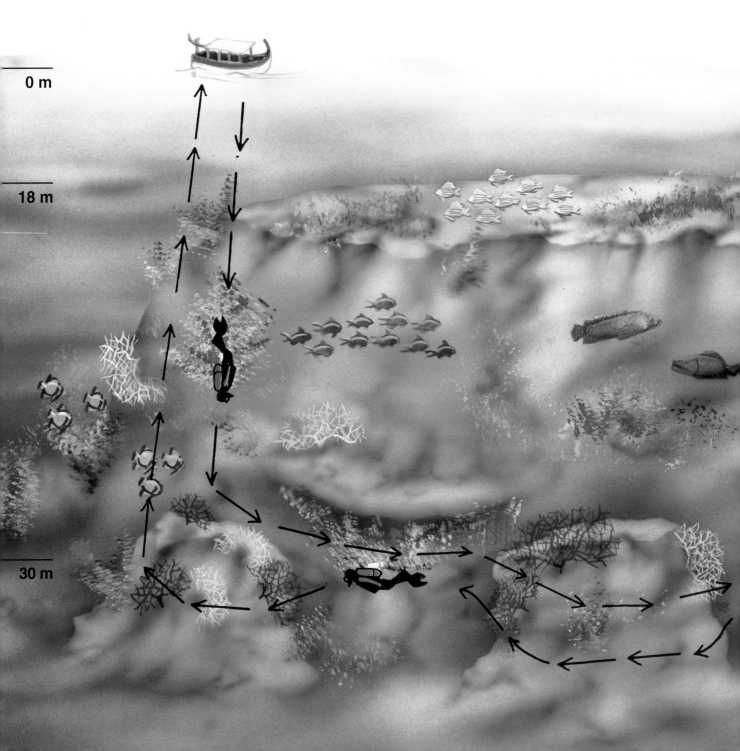

0 m

18 m

30 m

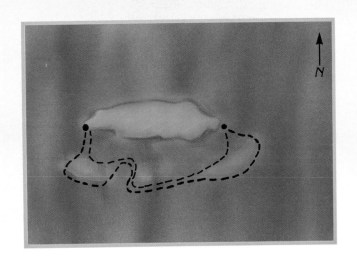

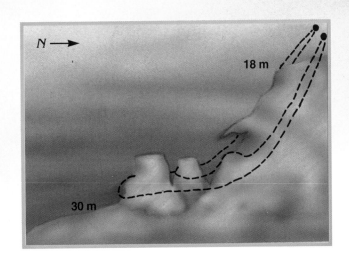

LOCATION

Blue Canyon is situated on the western side of the North Malé Atoll. Nearby islands are Ziyaaraiyfushi to the south and Makunudhoo to the east, both of which have tourist resorts. The diving area is a shoal which is rather difficult to identify, as its summit is situated 18 meters deep. On the south side of the *thila*, several large coral formations not far from the wall form a true canyon 30 meters deep. At this point on the floor, the wall of the shoal is punctuated by deep recesses. From the roof of these canopies hang splendid thick bunches of blue-lilac and yellow alcyonarians.

DESCRIPTION OF THE DIVE

As this area is continually swept by powerful currents, you need to have good drift dive technique. You should enter the water about 50 meters above the shoal, checking the current, in order to have enough time for the descent. Once you reach the southern side of the coral foundation, all you need to do is let yourself be carried by the current into the canyon, from time to time taking shelter behind the jutting projections in the wall. The dive ends in the deep sea with safety decompression in the open water. The interior of the canyon is

A and B - Thick clusters of rare violet alcyonarians hang from the top of this crevice. Also note the numerous formations of Tubastrea *coral with its polyps retracted.*

C - A diver observes the vertical walls of the reef; in the foreground are large branches of gorgonian sea-fans.

D - Dense clusters of yellow sea-fans in the genus Acabaria *embellish this wall, near which several butterflyfish hover.*

a true explosion of colors, with the ice white to violet roofs and walls of the grottos. You will see large yellow and red sea fans on the sides of the large coral mushrooms that rise from the sand. Here it is common to see whitetip sharks resting on the sea bed, with their snouts turned toward the current. Fissures in the reef shelter groups of soldierfish, anthias and glassfish moving in formation. Numerous red groupers *(Cephalopoholis miniata)* peep out of their dens. Looking carefully at the hard coral formations, you may identify numerous pairs of longnose filefish *(Oximonacanthus longirostris)*, continuously chasing each other in a ballet of jerks and

G

E - A sea turtle (Eretmochelis imbricata), completely unintimidated by human presence, rests peacefully on the protuberances of the wall.

F - Another inhabitant of small caves is the Oriental sweetlips (Plecthorhynchus orientalis). A cleaner fish (Labroides bicolor) can be seen above the sweetlips.

G - These glassfish (Parapriacanthus guentheri) appear before the diver like a wall of silvery reflections.

H - Within the cavities of the reef there are always dense schools of blotcheye soldierfish (Myripristis murdjan), with their brilliant red scales.

E

F

H

abrupt stops. You are likely to encounter some fine examples of sea turtles during the dive, and on top of the shoal are dense schools of bluestriped snappers *(Lutjanus kasmira)* swimming in compact formation. Given its position, quite exposed to currents flowing in and out of the atoll, there could always be a surprise encounter in this area. As it is difficult to locate the exact point of entry, you should rely on particularly skilled boatmen and divemasters, especially in evaluating the strength of the current.
It is absolutely necessary to use the signal buoy, as divers can travel great distances in the five minutes that pass from the time

they leave the bottom to the time they reach the surface.

PHOTOGRAPHY

The roofs of the grottos with their deep blue alcyonarians can frame a beautiful photo with a scuba diver at the water's surface. Don't forget to aim the flash upwards. You can use medium angle lenses to get good photos of the schools of snappers and of turtles resting on the reef.

KAGI GIRI

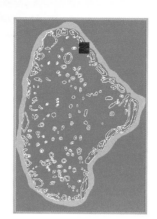

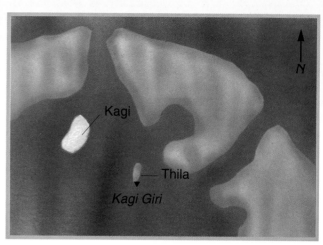

0 m

30 m

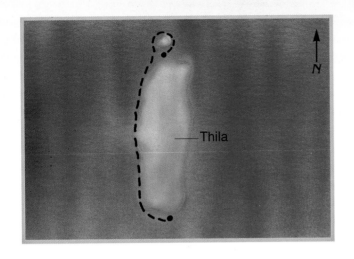

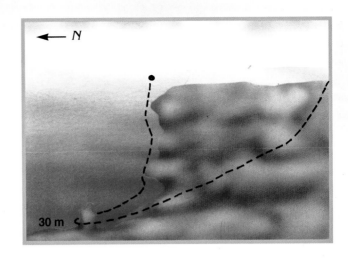

A - Predators are most active at night, and every species at risk adopts its own strategy of defense. When parrotfish, for example, take shelter for the night, they excrete a protective mucus from their mouths that covers them completely. The photo shows an Indian steepheaded parrotfish (Scarus strongylocephalus) intent on this operation.

B - A coral goby rests comfortably on a coral branch. In the event of danger, this little animal seeks refuge within the tangled corals, becoming impossible to catch.

LOCATION

The Kagi Giri is situated in the northern part of the North Malé Atoll, within the coral reef that traces the borders of the atoll. The closest islands are the desert island of Kagi, with Helengeli a little farther to the south, where there is a tourist village. The diving point is a round *giri* that rises from a depth of about 27-30 meters almost to the surface. The wall facing the northwest contains numerous small grottos, and two mushroom formations detached from the coral table rise from the sandy bottom.

DESCRIPTION OF THE DIVE

The most interesting side of the shoal is certainly the one facing north. Keeping in mind that there are practically no currents in this area, you should begin the dive in the northern part, which is also the deepest. Once you have reached the

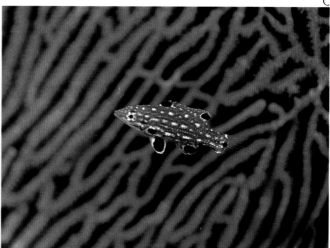

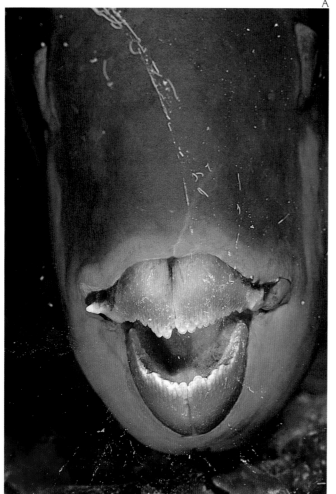

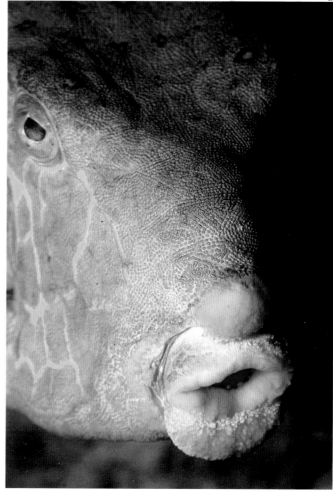

C - A small wrasse tries to camouflage itself among the branches of a sea-fan, taking advantage of its mimetic colors.

D - Cube boxfish (Ostracion cubicus) are very shy, and can usually only be approached at night. With their rather awkward movements, they are one of the strangest inhabitants of the reef.

E - A sea plume is a rare encounter for divers. It is not easy to spot these strange animal, both because by day they are curled up and appear to be dry branches, and because they live on the sandy seabeds usually ignored by divers.

desired depth, follow the wall, keeping it to your left, and begin to come back up to the edge of the partially submerged reef. This shoal is also a good diving area during the day, but it is truly at its best at night.

All the creatures that by day usually hide within the numerous cavities that speckle the reef come out at dusk to feed, making this *giri* a true kaleidoscope of colors. By night the wall of Kagi Giri is a veritable explosion of color. The light of underwater torches rekindles the colors of all the coral forms, which never seem as brilliant by day. Camouflaged spider crabs wander through the red-orange sea fans, while clownfish peep out of the stinging tentacles of the sea anemones. All the polyps of the alcyonarians and other reef builders expand and contract rhythmically as they feed on the plankton.

In the recesses of the walls are red soldierfish *(Myripristis sp.).* After sunset even the lobsters come out into the open and can

easily be seen as they move about on the reef. Drowsing in the more sheltered areas, the parrotfish secrete a protective mucus from their mouths with which they completely cover themselves to avoid being detected by nocturnal predators that hunt by scent. Mollusks move on the sandy floor, as do cowries, with their mantles turned outwards to completely cover their shells. You may also encounter sea turtles resting on small terraces on the reef.

Night dives are fascinating and pleasurable as long as you pay attention to detail. Before it grows dark, you should set a floating strobe at the edge of the shoal so that you can easily identify the point where you will enter the water. A signal light should always be attached to the valves of the air tank so that you can be identified, and you should carry an emergency underwater lamp.

F - A small blenny takes refuge in this hard coral formation, where it peeps out of its den with its mouth open in a sign of challenge.

G - A delicate, brilliant pink nudibranch moves slowly along the wall of the coral reef.

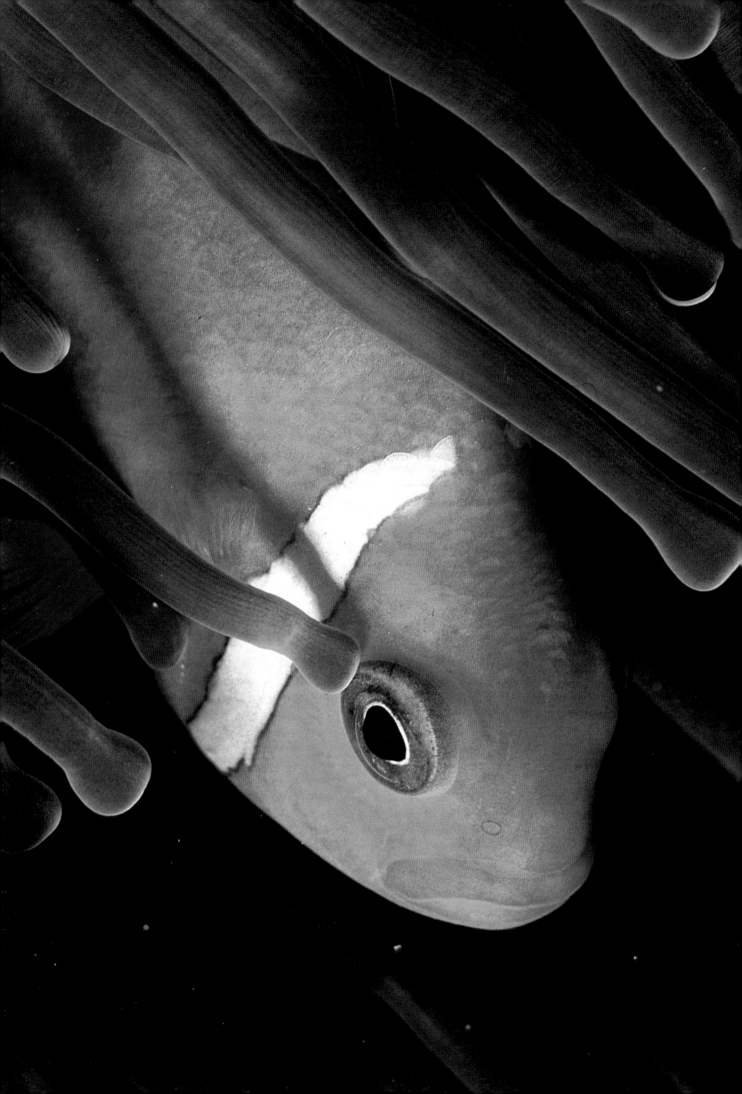

PHOTOGRAPHY

This shoal is a true paradise for those who love close-up photos. Equipment that can be used includes anything from extension tubes, with various enlargement ratios, to a close-up lens. For best results, use cameras in an underwater case with 60 or 105 millimeter micro lenses. The expanded coral polyps, perhaps with a small fish nearby, will be excellent subjects. By positioning the flash to TTL mode, you will be free to concentrate on framing the shot.

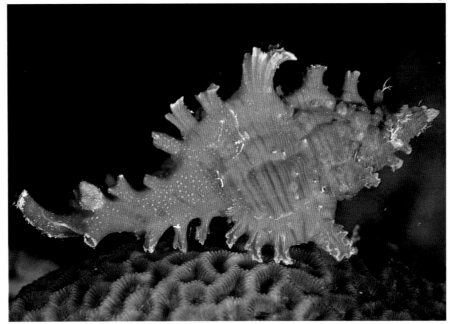

A - This black-footed clownfish (Amphiprion nigripes) feels safely among the tentacles of the sea anemone. These extremely territorial fish spend their entire lives associated with the same anemone.

B - Life on the coral reef goes on without interruption at night. The polyps of the alcyonarians, such as this Dendronephyta-type, expand in order to catch the plankton on which they feed.

C - Numerous species of crustaceans live among the branches of alcyonarians, where they find shelter and food. Here we see a tiny crab (Naxioides taurus) about two centimeters long.

D - This gastropod stands out due to its bright orange shell.

E - This "pajama" nudibranch, so called due to its particular coloring, is resting on a red sponge.

VAH KANDU

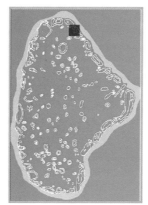

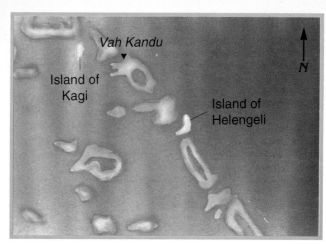

Island of Kagi

Vah Kandu

Island of Helengeli

N

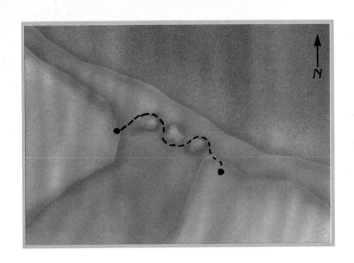

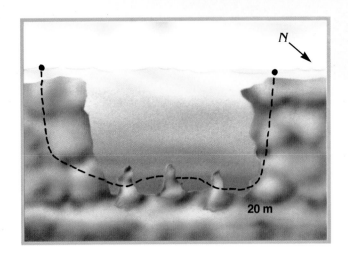

LOCATION

Vah Kandu is situated at the far northeast side of the Malé Atoll. West of the pass is the desert island of Kagi with its lovely lagoon, and farther south is the tourist island of Helengeli. The diving area is outside of the channel on the shelf of the oceanic reef, which reaches a depth of 20-25 meters. Three pinnacles 3-4 meters in height rise from the relatively flat plateau, marking the entry to the channel proper. This is the narrowest pass I have ever dived into in the Maldives, with its two vertical walls only 15-20 meters apart. The sandy bottom of the channel is about 18 meters deep.

DESCRIPTION OF THE DIVE

This dive should be made when there is no current, so that you can stay on the outside shelf during your entire down-time without being pushed too quickly to the inside of the atoll.
Enter the water on one of the two outer oceanic walls, and after having reached the appropriate depth, stay near the mushroom formations at the entry to the pass. When you decide to emerge, it is best to do so by entering the channel and following one of the two side walls to the surface.
As in all dives outside the atolls, here it is also possible to see migratory fish such as tunas and

A - Along the inner walls of the oceanic channels it is easy to meet turtles swimming in the open water as they follow the current.

B - The oceanic passes are the best places to encounter large pelagians. Gray sharks are a certainty when diving at Vah Kandu.

C - Two different species of crinoids can be seen attached to this branch of black coral (Antipathes sp.). The base of the trunk is, on the other side, colonized by red sponges.

D - A group of red-tailed butterflyfish (Chaetodon collare) moves tranquilly, not at all intimidated by the divers, who can observe them from close up.

whitetip sharks and barracudas. Usually there is a group of eagle rays suspended between the surface and the pinnacles at the entry to the channel.

Schools of jacks swimming in circular fashion are quite common in the corners of the pass. You are also likely to see numerous turtles, probably because the nearby island of Kagi is one of the very few places on the atoll where these animals come to deposit their eggs. Inside the pass you will find many types of butterflyfish, from the red-tailed butterflyfish to bannerfish. It is inadvisable to dive in this area when there are strong currents entering the atoll, turbulence and

F

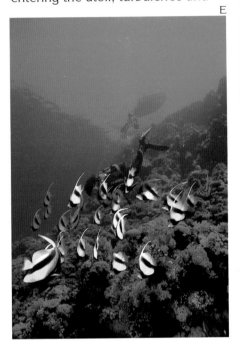

E

G

vertical currents are created in the narrow funnel of the channel which could cause problems.

PHOTOGRAPHY

Lenses such as the 28 mm and the 20 mm *Nikonos* are recommended for shots of the eagle rays without coming too close to the subjects, or for jacks, and full frame shots of sharks. Divers with a reflex in an underwater case will obtain excellent results by mounting a zoom on the camera such as a 28-70.

E - A diver who has just entered the water finds himself in the midst of a group of bannerfish (Heniochus diphreutes), recognizable by their long dorsal fins.

F - A silvery mass of elegant barracudas (Sphyraena sp.) surrounds a diver like a whirlpool in the portion of the Vah Channel that opens into the lagoon.

G - Large schools of carangids like these bigeye trevallies (Caranx sexfasciatus) darting before the photographer, gather in areas where the current is more powerful.

49

LHAVIYANI ATOLL

It is separated from the Kaafu Atoll by the Kashidhoo Channel and is about six hours by *dhoni* north of Malé. It extends 35 miles north to south and 36 miles east to west. The population of the atoll is about 10,200 inhabitants. Capital island is Naifaru, located on the western edge of the atoll. The population of Naifaru is about 4,100 inhabitants. It is a very busy port. Good fishing ground. Only five islands are inhabited, rest of the islands are not inhabited.

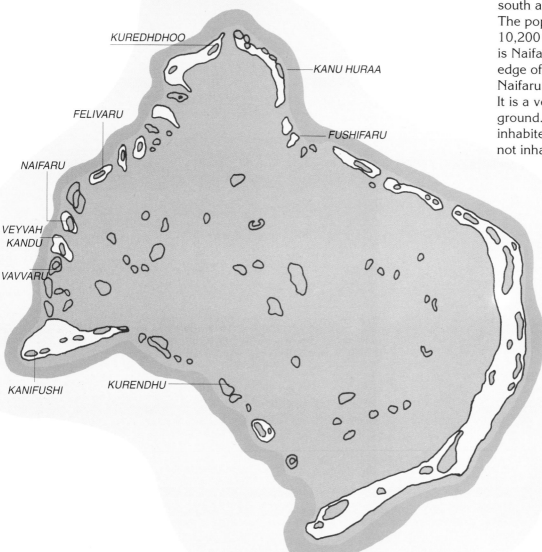

KUREDHDHOO
KANU HURAA
FELIVARU
FUSHIFARU
NAIFARU
VEYVAH KANDU
VAVVARU
KANIFUSHI
KURENDHU

A

Hinnavaru, about as big as Naifaru, is quite prosperous due to tourism and the fishing industry.
Felivaru has a canned tuna industry that employs a lot of inhabitants of the atoll.
The only tourist island is **Kuredhdhoo**, about 80 miles from Malé. It has the largest tourist village in the Maldives, under Swedish management, with 500 beds.

A - These indentations in the reef are excellent natural ports where boats can moor for the night or spend the day for relaxation and snorkeling.

B - Fishermen return to port in the early afternoon with their catch. Tunas are the primary prey and are always caught using fishing poles, the only type of fishing permitted in the Maldives.

C - The crystal clear waters are truly inviting. Tropical seas like the Red Sea and the waters around the Maldives are the best places to try scuba diving for the first time, perhaps by taking a beginner's course.

D - A dhoni floating motionlessly on the calm waters near an island of fishermen. Note the long fishing poles resting against the mainmast.

E - The Koi Malaa sailing through the shallow waters of the lagoon. The Koi Malaa is one of the most comfortable cruise boats in the Maldivian archipelago. Of quite recent construction, it is 23 meters long and has seven cabins with toilets and individual air conditioning: a real jewel.

VEYVAH KANDU

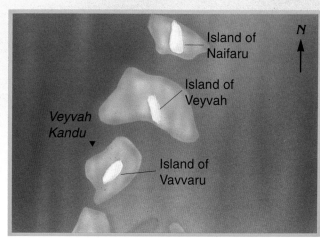

Island of
Naifaru

Island of
Veyvah

Veyvah
Kandu

Island of
Vavvaru

N

0 m

27 m

35 m

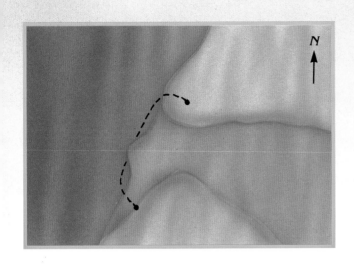

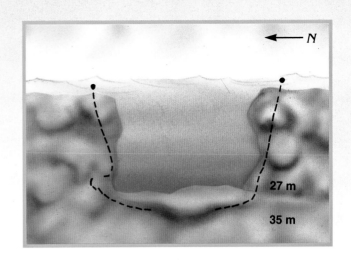

27 m

35 m

A - This portion of the reef is a true explosion of color; encrustations of alcyonarians, sponges and anthias create a many-hued picture.

B - The abundance of food brought in by the current encourages an extraordinary development of all types of corals.

LOCATION

Veyvah Kandu is situated on the western side of Lhaviyani. The neighboring islands of Vavvaru and Veivah are both uninhabited. A little farther north is the island of Naifaru, the capital of the atoll.
The diving area is the outside portion of the oceanic channel, with a drop-off that has a long offshoot in the center that thrusts out about 20 meters into the open sea.

A

B

DESCRIPTION OF THE DIVE

Enter the water from either corner of the pass. Be sure to check whether the current is flowing in or out, and make sure it is not running too fast. Once you reach the bottom, go to the end of the terrace, where you can explore the oceanic walls that drop vertically into the blue depths. Coming back to the walls of the oceanic reef, you can either enter the atoll or end the dive along the outside wall.
On the outside walls of this pass you will find some sea fans which are rather rare for the Maldivian archipelago, with brilliant colors ranging from bright red to yellow. Along the south wall there are several recesses adorned with alcyonarians and true trees of black coral. There is usually a school of jacks under the central drop-off, swimming in circular fashion. In the sandy portion of the channel, it is not uncommon to see a feathertail stingray *(Hypolophus sephen)*. This ray is easily identifiable by the end

C - The sandy and detritic areas of the reef are the reign of stingrays (Taeniura melanospilos), which prowl the flat expanses in search of food.

D - After female sea turtles reach maturity, they reproduce about once every two years, depositing 50 to 150 eggs in a hole dug in the beach which they later cover with sand. Incubation takes about two months.

portion of its tail. You will almost certainly encounter sea turtles, especially in shallower waters; perhaps they frequent the area because there are so many uninhabited islands where they can deposit their eggs. Numerous Oriental sweetlips *(Plectorhinchus orientalis)* gather along the wall north of the entry to the pass, around a coral formation that rises from the seabed.

During the winter season, perhaps due to the currents that carry in plankton, you may see one of the

most spectacular sights for a scuba diver, the whale shark. Apart from general safety rules valid for all dives in the pass, this dive is not particularly difficult and is suitable for divers with all levels of experience. If you decide to end the dive along the oceanic wall, you should surface at least 20 meters from the emerging reef to facilitate the movements of the diving *dhoni*.

PHOTOGRAPHY

The sea fans will certainly attract photographers, who can use wide-angle lenses to snap lovely images, with the colorful sea fans in the foreground. Using lenses such as a 28 millimeter you can get excellent shots of sweetlips or sea turtles.

E - In the open mouth of this sweetlips (Plectorhinchus orientalis) there is probably a cleaner shrimp, intent on his delicate dental work.

F - The beauty of these corals is equal to their fragility. All it takes is an unintentional blow from a diver's flippers to destroy years of work by the polyps.

FUSHI FARU KANDU

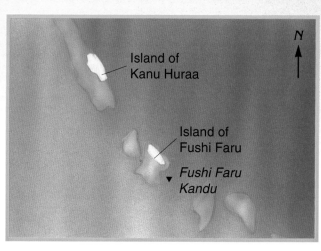

Island of
Kanu Huraa

Island of
Fushi Faru

*Fushi Faru
Kandu*

N

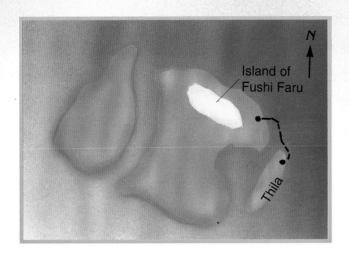

Island of
Fushi Faru

Thila

N

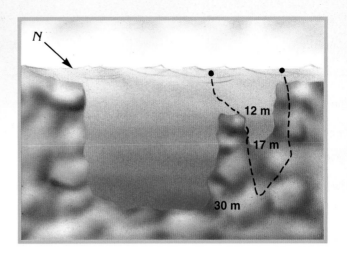

N

12 m

17 m

30 m

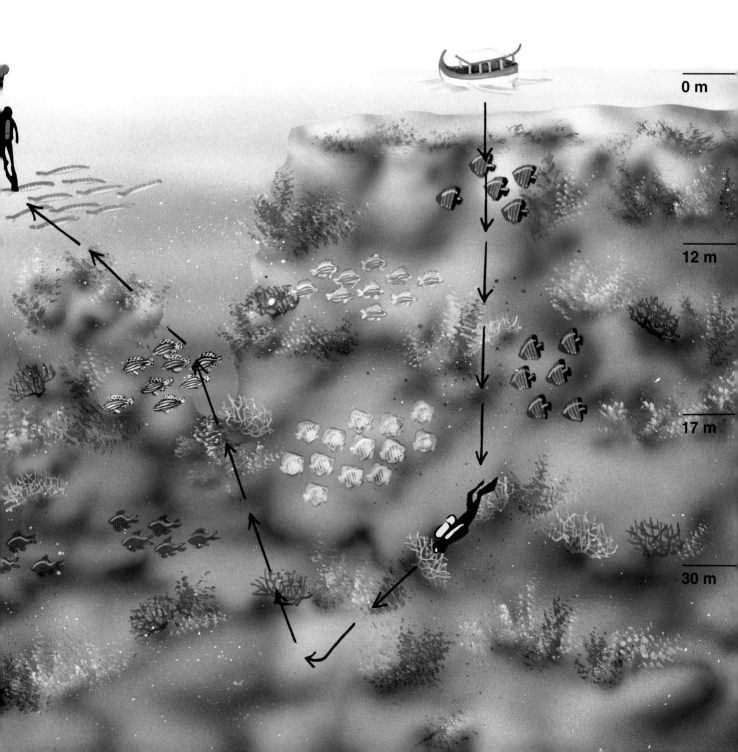

0 m

12 m

17 m

30 m

A - A group of red-tailed butterflyfish (Chaetodon collare) swims close to the reef. The fish are probably perlusrating the coral formations in order to find some food.

B - This shot of a manta ray, was taken in natural lighting to highlight the subject's characteristic silhouette against the sun.

LOCATION

Fushi Faru is situated on the northeastern side of Lhaviyani. Nearby islands, both of which are uninhabited, are Fushi Faru and Kanuhuraa. To be exact, it is located in the northern corner of the pass, with an outside drop-off at a depth of 30 meters. Within the channel, located near the north wall, is a humped coral formation which runs from east to west. This sort of *thila* has a southern wall which drops vertically to the bottom of the pass, while the northern wall links up almost to the reef and forms a canyon 18 meters deep.

DESCRIPTION OF THE DIVE

Enter the water, preferably with a weak incoming current, along the ocean wall north of the opening of the pass. Descending vertically, you will reach a broad terrace at a depth of 30 meters, and after pushing to the edge of the drop-off,

A

B

return toward the wall and begin rising along the northern corner of the channel. When you are at a depth of about 17 meters, you will see a vast formation of stinging corals *(Millepora sp.)*. Cutting slightly to the left, you will come to the crest of the shoal. Once you have explored the area at a depth of between 15 and 12 meters, leave the bottom, and while you make the safety stop at 5 meters deep, send the buoy to the surface so that you can be located and picked up by the *dhoni*.

In the deeper area of the dive you may meet stingrays swimming on the detrital floor and several large humphead wrasses that eye skin-divers warily. Looking up, you may see small groups of barracudas, hovering in the current, and eagle rays, usually in pairs.

The most spectacular part of the dive is nevertheless the interior of the pass, where along the ridge that pushes into the atoll are large schools of red-tailed butterflyfish *(Chetodon collare)*,

C - Several pinnacles, surrounded by frenetic activity, rise from the seabed in the corner that marks the pass.

E

F

D

D - This photo shot using the backlighting technique shows a humpback wrasse (Cheilinus undulatus), which was illuminated with the flash in order to give color to the image.

E - Several Oriental sweetlips (Plectorhinchus orientalis) have found shelter under this Acropora umbrella of. Corals in the Acropora genus grow very quickly, up to 20-25 centimeters a year.

bluestriped snappers *(Lutjanus kasmira)* and Oriental sweetlips *(Plectorhinchus orientalis).* These groups of fish with their various markings form true "balls" of color that make this dive one of the most spectacular of the entire atoll. Dense colonies of multi-colored alcyonarians have found an ideal habitat on the top of the coral formation. During the summer, this zone becomes an enormous grooming station for the manta rays, which can be seen while they stop half submerged in the water so the little cleaner wrasses *(Labloides dimidiatus)* can remove skin parasites.
This is a dive suitable for all levels of experience. Just keep your position under control and know how to handle a drift dive.
Apart from cruise boats, this area is frequented only by customers of the Kuredu Diving-School. Resort instructors, ably directed by Steffan and Alfons, are very sensitive to environmental

protection, and they are always careful to explain how scuba divers can avoid damaging the reef, with the result that the entire area is still almost completely intact.

PHOTOGRAPHY

Using 28 and 20 millimeter lenses, you can take good photographs of schools of fish in the saddle in the middle of the pass. As a rule, you should try to frame them from below, to give the picture more depth and avoid collapsing the perspective. Using extreme wide-angle lenses from 16 to 18 millimeters, you can take full frame shots of a good portion of the *thila* with all its inhabitants.

F - The yellow scales of the bluestriped snappers (Lutjanus kasmira) are crossed by four horizontal blue stripes. When these fish swim in very compact groups, it is quite difficult to tell one individual from another and to thus successfully attack them.

BAA ATOLL

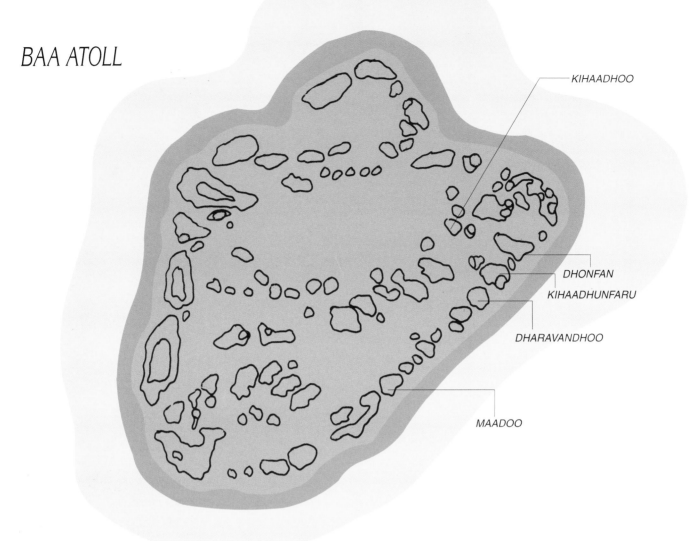

KIHAADHOO

DHONFAN

KIHAADHUNFARU

DHARAVANDHOO

MAADOO

The Baa Atoll is geographically situated along the chain of atolls facing west. On the south, it borders the small island of Goidhoo and to the north is separated from the Raa Atoll by the Moresby Channel. In Divehi its name is South Maalhosmadulu. Baa extends 33 miles north to south and 25 miles east to west.
Only 13 islands are inhabited, and almost all are located on the eastern side; the capital is Eydhafushi, which is 64 miles from Malé, an active fishing port which was once famous for its weavers of cotton feyli.
Dharavandhoo is quite a large island, with numerous fruit trees and a busy shipyard.

Thulhaadhoo is famous for its lacquered earthenware products, which provide employment for the entire village.
There is only one tourist resort in the entire atoll, **Sonevafushi**, which is located on the large Island of Kunfunadhoo.
Baa is one of the most interesting cruise destinations, not only because of its authentic indigenous villages, but also because of its truly splendid desert islands: **Viyafushi**, with a lagoon so deep that boats can be moored directly on the beach; **Kudadhoo**, with a lagoon which is home to a school of dolphins that often swims around moored boats at sunrise; and **Giraavaru**, with its splendid beach.

A

A - The islands on the Baa Atoll are extremely large compared with the average size of most Maldivian islands.

B - The coral reefs are a paradise not only for diving, but also for snorkeling. In just a few meters of water you can see all the many-colors of the reef.

C - On the atolls far from the capital, life goes on tranquilly, following rhythms governed by natural events like the rising and setting of the sun.

D - The traditional and the modern face to face. In the foreground is the stern of a dhoni *with its characteristic helm; behind it is the Huvani, a comfortable cruise boat with 6 cabins, all with bathrooms and large common areas.*

E - Only one tourist resort exists on the entire atoll: Sonevafushi. It is a rather exclusive village which tourists can reach by a Hummingbird helicopter.

*F - A diver is following a group of silver batfish (*Platax sp.*), fascinating inhabitatnts of the Maldivian underwater paradise.*

GIRAAVARU CORNER

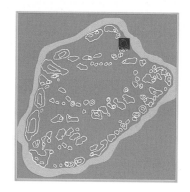

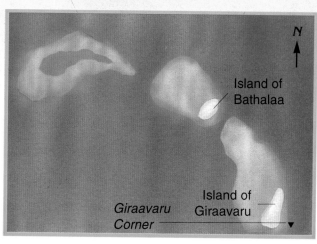

Island of
Bathalaa

Giraavaru
Corner

Island of
Giraavaru

N

0 m

5 m

30 m

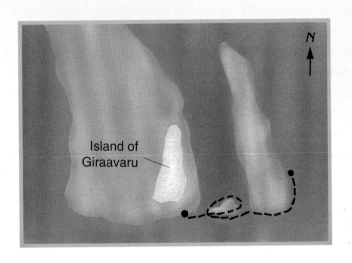

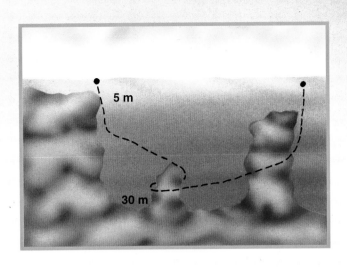

5 m

30 m

Island of
Giraavaru

N

LOCATION

Giraavaru is located in the northeastern area of the Baa Atoll. It is the northern corner of the very wide channel that separates the northern part of the Baa Atoll. At this point the oceanic wall outside the atoll and near the pass seems to have been chopped in two, thus forming a false second outside wall. This, similar to an emerging *giri*, runs for more than a hundred meters parallel to and about 10 meters from the coast. The actual entry to the pass can be identified by a large isolated coral formation about 20 meters in diameter. Water depth between the wall and the saddle is from 25 to 30 meters, while on the outside, after an initial drop to 30 meters, the waters plunge to unfathomable depths. Nearby islands are Giraavaru and Bathalaa, a little farther to the north.

DESCRIPTION OF THE DIVE

At Giraavaru you can decide whether to dive into the canyon or to explore the area outside it. In both cases the dive ends within the atoll itself, under the island's reef, where you will see numerous coral mushrooms surrounded by great numbers of the colorful, lively inhabitants of the reef. In any event, you should wait for an incoming tide for best visibility. In this dive, which is very pleasant and suitable for scuba divers of all levels, you may find a number of whitetip sharks near the outside wall of the saddle as they peacefully cross near the corner of the pass. Large sea fans, some of them a beautiful bright red, are attached to jutting ledges, with groups of blue fusiliers tranquilly swimming around them. If you go into the canyon, you will see stingrays intently inspecting the sandy bottom in search of the mollusks and small crustaceans on which they feed. When you reach the isolated coral mushroom you may see schools of red-tailed butterflyfish *(Chaetodon*

C - This sea-fan, growing in a crack in the reef, offers a hold for several crinoids, which filter the water through their plumed arms in order to feed.

D - Two sweetlips (Plectorhinchus orientalis) have infiltrated a group of red-tailed butterflyfish (Chaetodon collare). It is not uncommon to find these mixed groups near the surface in areas where the current is weak.

E - This brilliant bloom of alcyonarians gives a red tinge to a slope on which small groups of bluestriped snappers (Lutjanus kasmira) move.

F - The blue ribbon eel (Rhinomuraena quaesita) is the only moray that changes color and sex as it grows. It is not easy to spot, as it retreats into its hole at any suspect movement or noise. This photo shows the blue coloring typical of adults of the species.

G - A diver moves toward a branch of sea-fan around which hundreds of small Indian flame basslet (Pseudanthias ignitus) swim.

collare), swimming near the bottom in compact formations, and a little forest of black coral. In this area you may encounter a number of blue ribbon eels *(Rhinomurenae quasitae)*. This is the only species of moray that changes color and sex during its lifetime. Young ones, up to 60 centimeters long, are black with a very fine yellow dorsal fin, then they mature as males, with a beautiful cornflower blue color and a more pronounced yellow dorsal fin.
At about 1 meter in length they become female and turn completely yellow. As you finish your dive in the shallow waters of the reef, you will see parrotfish, angelfish and butterflyfish swimming peacefully through the corals.
As always when you dive in a completely virgin area such as this, you need to be more careful than usual, as the entire reef is pulsing with life, and any contact with it would cause damage to the tiny colonies of polyps that form it.

G

E

F

H

PHOTOGRAPHY

All types of lenses can be used for this dive. Use a wide-angle lens to photograph the sea fans and branches of black coral.
With the 28 and 25 mm you can get good shots of the schools of colorful butterflyfish.
You will need an amphibious macro optical system to catch the small and timid morays, who will retreat to their dens if you come too close.

H - The double-saddled butterflyfish (Chaetodon falcula) is the classic butterflyfish of the Indian Ocean. It lives in pairs, but occasionally gathers in groups of about twenty individuals. It is easy to approach.

DHONFAN THILA

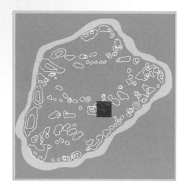

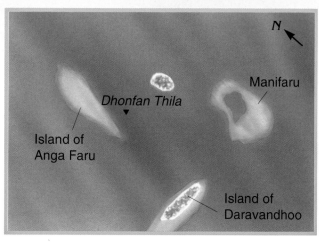

Island of
Anga Faru

Dhonfan Thila

Manifaru

Island of
Daravandhoo

N

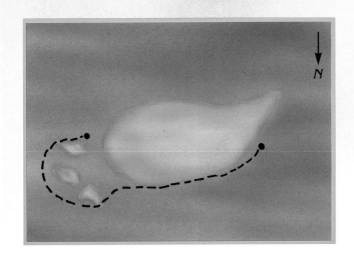

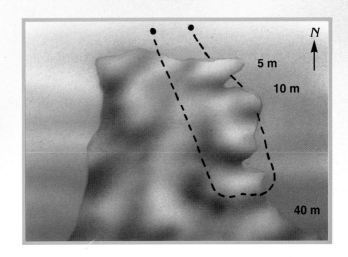

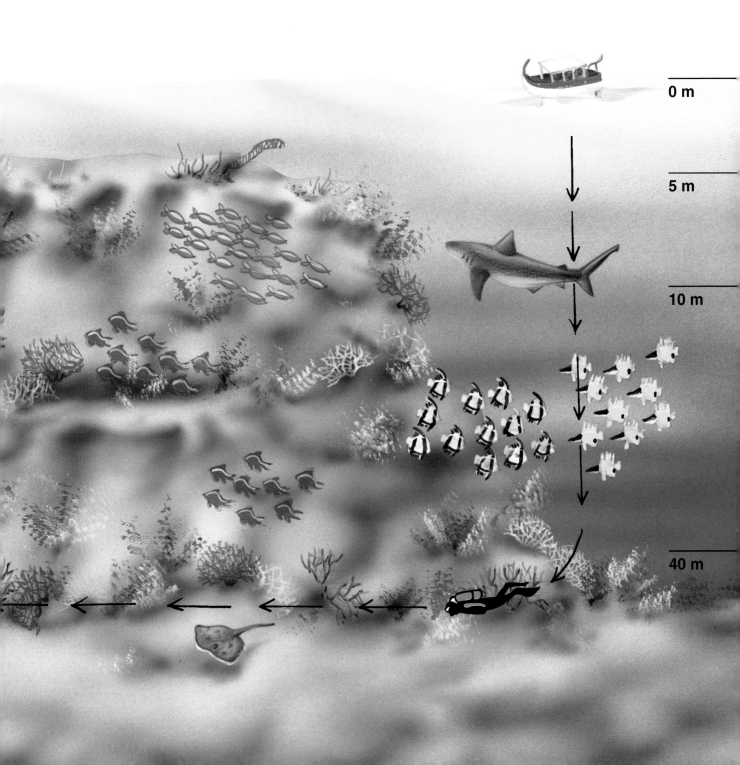

LOCATION

The Dhonfan Thila is situated in the east central area of the Baa Atoll, exactly halfway to the Anga reef. This shoal, the top of which is 5 meters from the surface, has an elongated form running from east to west. On the eastern side there are several large detached coral masses, and the wall is full of grottos. The sandy bottom goes from a depth of 30 to 40 meters.

DESCRIPTION OF THE DIVE

As this *thila* is located some way within the atoll, the currents are not very strong, thus making it an easy, tranquil and very pleasant dive. Divers usually enter the water on the eastern side near the large coral rocks. After exploring these pinnacles, proceed with the dive, keeping the wall of the reef to your left, and end by coming up on the top of the reef.

This is one of the most beautiful places in the atoll, both due to the numerous schools of sedentary fish you may encounter and to the rich forms and colors of the coral. Don't forget that this place is accessible to cruise boats only, and very few guides know its exact location. A large school of jacks is always present at the summit of the pinnacles; it is easy to approach them as they swim slowly in circular fashion.

A -
The photographer is selecting the best frame to take a shot of a school of jacks (Caranx sexfasciatus) *from below, probably with backlighting.*

B - Fusiliers (Caesio xanthonota) *sometimes gather in schools so dense that they block the light of the sun.*

C -
Macrophotography let you admire closely the delicate structure of a red gorgonian branch.

D - At the base of the Dhonfan reef one may encounter dense groups of snappers (Lutjanus kasmira), *which often swim in circular fashion one after the other.*

Enormous groups of yellow and blue yellowfin fusiliers (Caesio xanthonota) are permanent guests, and you may easily encounter another resident of the base of the shoal: a majestic sharkfin guitarfish, which you may approach taking the appropriate precautions. You may also see gray sharks swimming peacefully in the blue waters and stingrays resting on the sandy bottom. This area is particularly lovely due to the explosion of life that covers the walls: alcyonarians in a thousand colors, large sea fans and trees of black coral. With a bit a luck, on the top of the thila you may see the den of a zebra moray. Given the great number of coral

E

formations it is impossible to find any space to lean on, so a good neutral position is absolutely necessary, especially for photographers.

PHOTOGRAPHY

The large isolated colorful alcyonarians and branches of black coral offer good possibilities for very impressive photos, either against the light or with a diver in the background. You can take excellent, brightly colored seascapes using a wide-angle lens.

G - This solitary, timid zebra moray (Gymnomuranea zebra) feeds primarily on small crustaceans. It is most easy to find at night, when it comes out in search of food.

H - In the Baa Atoll, and especially in the Dhonfan area, there are varieties of larger than average sea-fans in extraordinarily brilliant colors.

I - Illuminated by the flash, these glassfish reflect the light like a golden waterfall.

F

G

E - Thanks to their delicate shape, the alcyonarians growing along the vertical wall of the reef at Dhonfan, give us breathtaking underwater scenes.

F - This pair of bannerfish (Heniochus diphreutes) swims near the seabed in its daily search for the zooplankton that makes up its primary diet.

H

I

MAADDOO GIRI

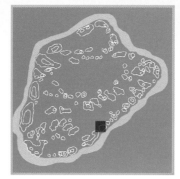

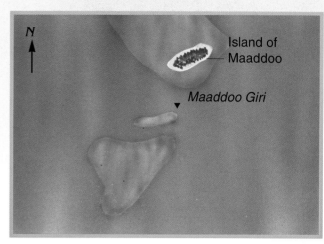

0 m

4 m

25 m

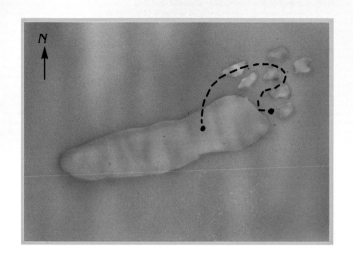

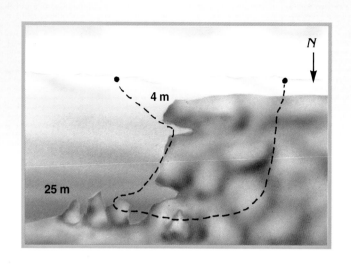

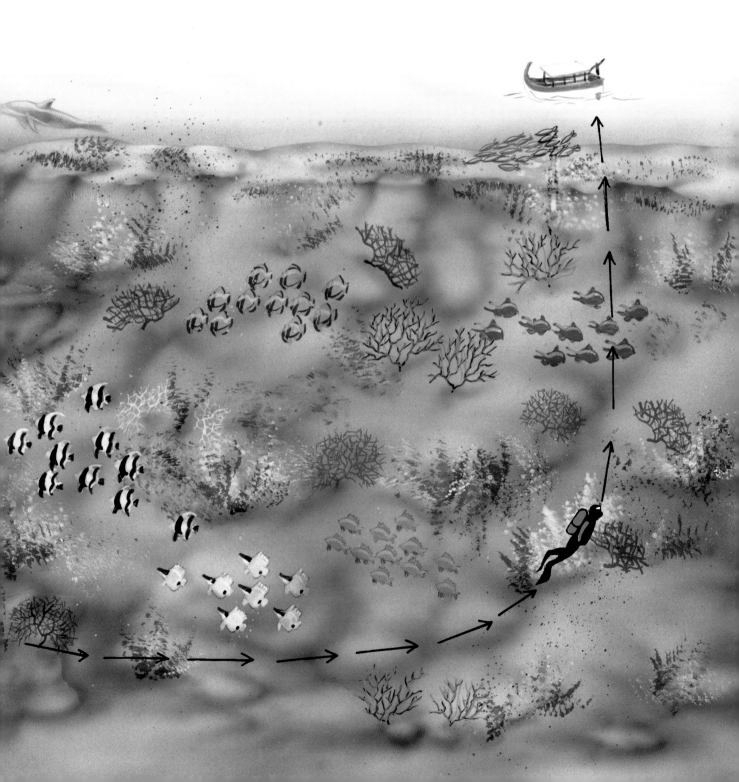

A - The habit of gathering in compact schools is one of the defense systems of small fish, who are thus able to confuse their predators. The photo shows a group of yellow fusilierfish (Caesio xanthonota).

B - Sea-fans in spectacular forms and colors grow on the north wall of the giri; these octocorals have a horny skeleton which is usually covered with a softer sheath.

C

A

D

B

C - This tree of black coral grows vigorously on a protuberance on the wall. Unregulated gathering has caused its near disappearance in some areas of the Maldives.

D - An enormous school of jacks (Caranx sp.) moves away as a group of divers approaches.

LOCATION

The Maaddoo Shoal is located on the eastern edge of the Baa Atoll in the oceanic channel between the Island of Maaddoo and the Hulhudhoo Reef. The *giri* rises from a depth of over 40 meters to 4 meters from the surface and extends for about 150 meters in a slightly elongated form. In the eastern part, where dives usually begin, masses of coral have slid in a vaguely Mediterranean formation, which goes from a depth of 25 meters from the surface to the sea floor, creating quite an unusual environment for Maldivian seabeds.

DESCRIPTION OF THE DIVE

This is a rather difficult dive, first of all because powerful currents usually sweep through the area, making it necessary to carefully evaluate the exact point of entry into the water, and secondly because due to the crystal clear water it is easy to reach depths greater than those recommended for sport diving. Nevertheless, even when there are strong currents, the configuration of the seabed and the recesses in the wall form large areas where one can take shelter from the "liquid wind." The dive begins on the wall facing the open sea, and after exploring the large masses which have slid away, you may begin ascending along the wall to shallower depths. Safety decompression takes place in the open sea, where you are attached to the line of the signal buoy inflated at the end of the dive. Given the position and unusual form of the seabed, this shoal is one of the most spectacular on the atoll. Thousands of blue and yellow fusiliers form compact schools that move frenetically near the top of the *giri*. The reason for these rapid movements is the swift incursions into the school by large jacks and tunas, which cross the mass in great numbers. Enormous groups of bluestriped snappers *(Lutjanus kasmira)* and humpback red snappers *(Lutjanus gibbus)* swim among the broken masses

E, F - A large number of bluestriped snappers (Lutjanus kasmira) - photo top -, with their unmistakable yellow and blue coloring, and humpback red snappers (Lutjanus gibbus) - photo bottom -, with their brown backs and reddish sides, gather around the coral formations at the base of the reef.

on the seabed. Along the vertical walls near true black coral trees is the vibrating life typical of the reef wall, while elegant eagle rays glide through the blue depths. There is a rarity in this area: an enormous red sea fan attached to a spur of the wall. Dolphins often approach divers curiously as they are decompressing in the open sea, ending an already extraordinary dive with a flourish. As for all dives that require decompression in the open water, you should first be sure that you have the long line with the signal buoy in the pocket of the equilibrator jacket, so that it will reach the surface inflated and make it possible for the support *dhoni* to follow the movements of the diving group as they shift with the currents.

The shoal is not well known and is visited by very few divers. Consequently, the coral seabed is almost completely intact. If you need to stand on anything, you should use those small sandy areas on the bottom to avoid damaging the fragile reef ecosystem.

G

H

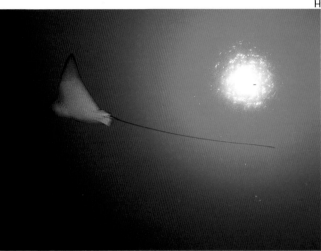

E

F

PHOTOGRAPHY

You can dive at Maaddoo dozens of times and never run out of things to photograph. The large groups of fish can be photographed using 20 to 28 millimeter lenses. Using super wide-angle lenses you can snap lovely seascapes, perhaps of the sea fans, with the form of a diver in the background. The hawkfish among the branches of the sea fans or resting on the corals are excellent subjects for those who prefer close-ups. Be sure to save a few photos for the end of the dive, as it would truly be a pity to be approached by a dolphin and have no film left to take a picture.

G - At the end of the dive near the top of the giri, one may encounter a few dolphins. Often one of the younger individuals will leave the school and come close to watch the divers.

H - The unmistakable form of an eagle ray rising toward the sunlight.

73

BAIYPOLHI MAS

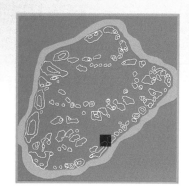

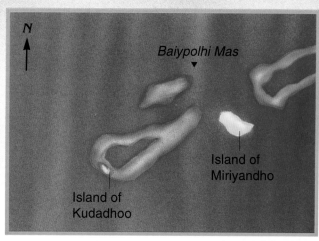

Island of Kudadhoo

Island of Miriyandho

Baiypolhi Mas

N

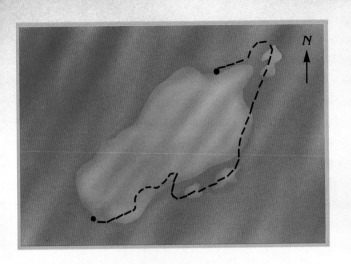

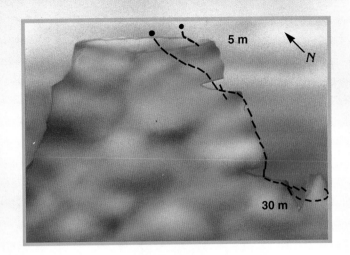

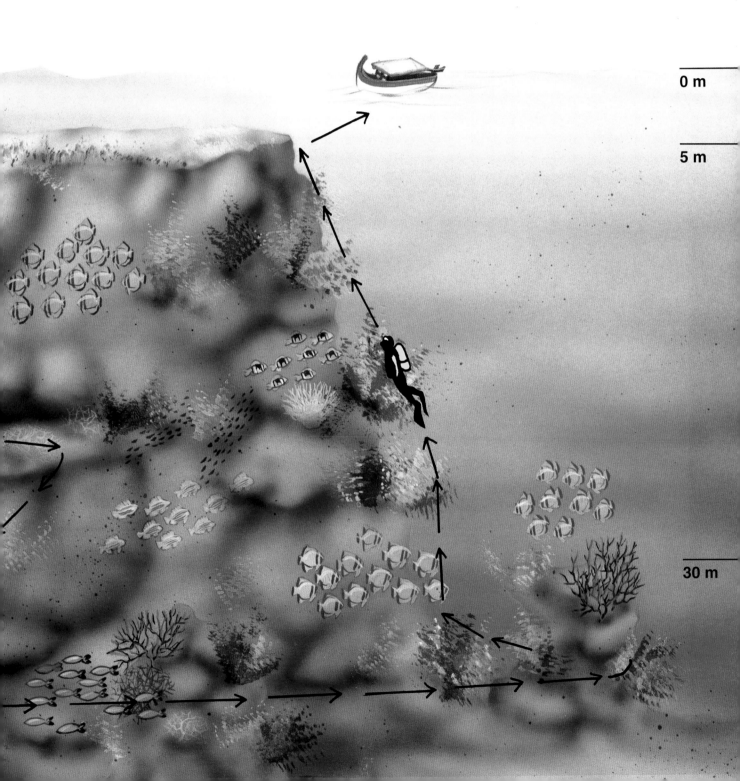

LOCATION

The Baiypolhi Mas Giri is situated in the emerging coral atoll in the pass between the islands of Kudadhoo and Miriyandhoo.
The top reef is at a depth of 5-7 meters, while the reef is about a hundred meters long and has a slightly elongated form. Its walls drop vertically to a depth of 32-37 meters, where the seabed is sandy with a few isolated coral formations.

DESCRIPTION OF THE DIVE

As this is a rather sheltered position, the *giri* is almost never subject to strong currents. In any event, you should note how fast the water is moving before you enter. It is better to dive with an inflowing current in order to have optimal visibility. This is how the "underwater tour" of the southeastern portion begins, where you will find deep horizontal cracks at a depth of 12 to 25 meters. After having explored several isolated masses on the floor, you may end your dive in the northern portion on the reef, where the diving *dhoni* will pick up divers.
In Dhivehi, the language spoken in the Maldives, Baiypolhi Mas means "batfish", and in fact the highest concentration of batfish *(Platax teira)* ever seen exists around this coral formation. You will encounter large schools of batfish swimming

at all depths. It is a truly unique spectacle to see these silvery white masses moving all together in a compact group. During the dive you will also see all the inhabitants of the reef, and several schools of bluestriped snappers *(Luijanus kasmira)*. True trees of black coral grow on the isolated masses on the seabed, along with enormous alcyonarians. In a recess in this formation lives a large, easily approachable, moray. Looking carefully on the seabed, it will be easy to see large stingrays half-buried in the sand. Sea-fans surrounded by soldierfish *(Myripristis sp.)* open up in the cracks in the wall. Encounters with scorpionfish are quite common on

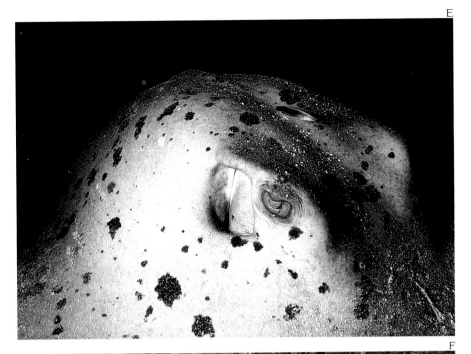

the top but you need to have a good eye, because, lying immobile on the bottom, they are well camouflaged. There are also numerous anemones inhabited by the usual clownfish.

PHOTOGRAPHY

This is certainly the place for a wide-angle lens, from the classic 15 mm *Nikonos* to more extreme amphibious optical systems, as the undisputed stars of this dive are the batfish. However, be careful with the flash: the scales of these fish reflect a great deal of light and it is not easy to obtain good images. It's better to use natural light and hold the flash up in your hand, to be used at some distance from the subject. Using the 80 mm lens and micro lenses in an underwater case, you can take good photos of the shrimp intent on cleaning the mouth of the moray, as well as good close-ups of scorpionfish.

A - A formation of batfish moves slowly toward the surface; their streamlined form makes it possible for them to remain immobile against the current.

B - The schools of batfish are always a fascinating sight. Both species, Platax orbicularis *and* Platax teira, *are present in the Maldives. These fish do not mind the presence of divers, even at close distance.*

C - Small groups of fusiliers ceaselessly traverse the shallower portion of the giri.

D - This rare soft coral has grown in a form that resembles a fir tree.

E - Even the large stingrays require the services of cleaner fish. Here is a cleaner wrasse (Labroides dimidiatus) *intent on cleaning the head of a ray.*

F - Three lionfish (Pterois miles) *seem to dance with their pectoral and dorsal fins fully extended in all their beauty.*

G - A moray peeps out of the entry to its den, where it passes most of the day, waiting for dark to come out to hunt.

GOIDHOO

Goidhoo is located on the western side of the archipelago, between the Baa and Ari Atolls.

It is an enormous coral ring that surrounds a deep lagoon, which can only be reached through a single pass located on the southern side of the uninterrupted reef: Dhorukandu. Facing the faru to the north are the only four islands of the atoll: **Innafushi**, **Fulhadhoo**, **Fehendhoo** and the more important **Goidhoo.** Although these four inhabited islands are isolated from the rest of the islands, they are administratively part of Baa Atoll. Due to the currents, which follow monsoon winds and which transport large quantities of plankton, dives around this small atoll can result in unusual encounters.

A curiosity: one day in February several years ago, four million flying fish leaped out of the water to die together on the shores of Goidhoo.

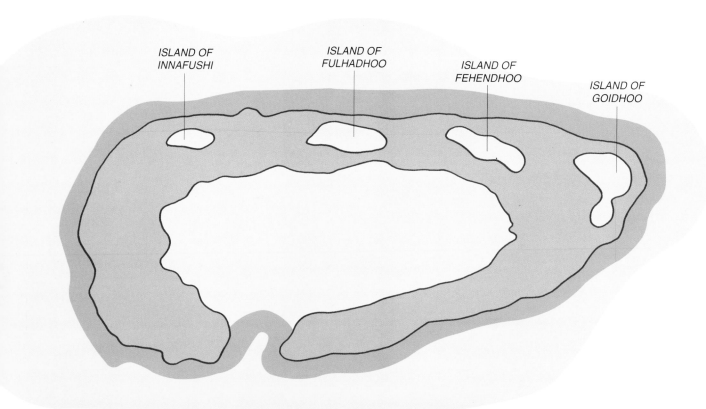

ISLAND OF
INNAFUSHI

ISLAND OF
FULHADHOO

ISLAND OF
FEHENDHOO

ISLAND OF
GOIDHOO

A

A - The large island of Goidhoo is the extreme eastern offshoot of the group of islands of the same name.

B - The constant breeze that sweeps across the Maldives makes it pleasant to sail even in small catamarans.

C - This picture shows the serene time divers can have on safari boats when they do not explore the underwater paradise of the Maldives.

D - Some dhonis are built of coconut palm wood using methods which have remained unchanged for hundreds of years.

E - A heron lies in wait motionlessly, waiting to catch a small fish with its long beak.

F - This aereal view shows clearly the reef conformation, that reaches almost the blue surface of the sea.

D

B

E

C

F

GOIDHOO OUTSIDE

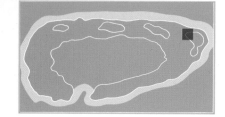

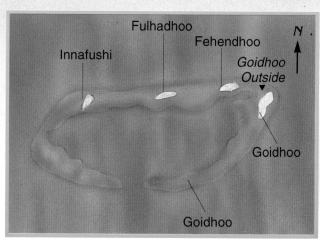

Innafushi   Fulhadhoo   Fehendhoo   *Goidhoo Outside*   N

Goidhoo

Goidhoo

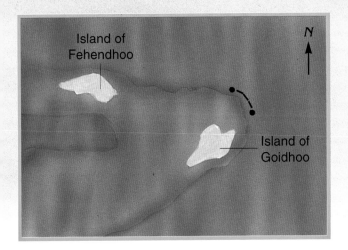

Island of
Fehendhoo

Island of
Goidhoo

N

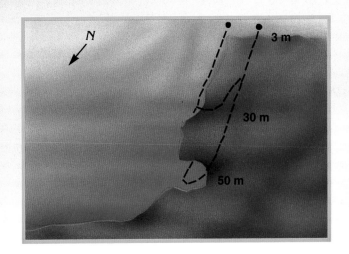

N

3 m

30 m

50 m

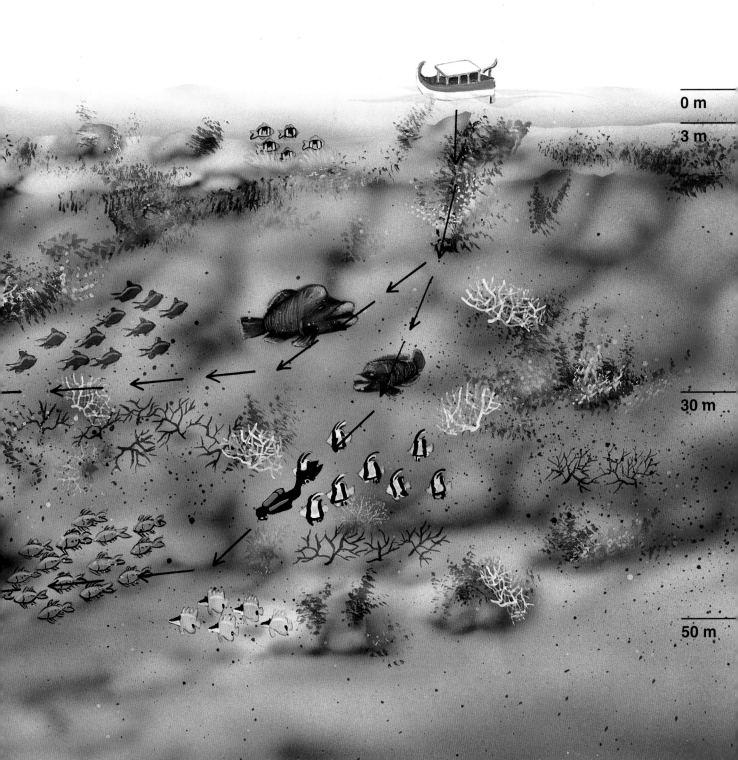

0 m

3 m

30 m

50 m

LOCATION

The diving area is situated on the northeast side of the Goidhoo outside the reef between the gorges of Goidhoo and Fehendhoo. This is a dive on the oceanic wall that begins at a depth of 3 meters and plunges into the sea to the first drop-off at 65 meters. The wall is vertically broken by a recess in the reef 2-3 meters wide and 6-7 meters deep. At a depth of about 50 meters there is a large, deep grotto and a number of isolated formations on the seabed.

DESCRIPTION OF THE DIVE

This dive is for very expert divers only, not just because of the strong currents that sweep the outside of the atoll, but also because of the depth you may reach due to the crystal clear water, which can be deceiving. Enter the water keeping the wall to your right, and let yourself be carried by the current while you descend. You may stop at a depth of 30-35 meters or go down to the cave 50 meters deep and end the dive inside the rift, which comes almost to the surface, and then to the reef for the safety stop at a depth of 4-5 meters while you wait under the balloon that signals our position to the boat.

This is also known as Red Wall, and it is the only area in the Maldives where a hard red-orange coral grows. The dive is certainly one of the most beautiful in the archipelago, not only because of the enormous branches of red coral that you can admire on the wall from a depth of about 30 meters on, but also because the reef is fully intact and uncontaminated. As it is exposed to northeast currents, the water is always crystal clear. You may easily encounter schools of barracudas that patrol the reef at a depth of about 30 meters, and a little below that there is always an enormous school of jacks swimming in circular fashion. Quite often there

A - The oceanic terrace, located about 30 meters deep, is embellished with a forest of red whip corals growing up toward the surface.

B - This dive is unique due to its large quantities of red Maldivian coral (Distichopora sp.) located at accessible depths.

C - Along the wall that plunges down into the depths grow enormous formations of brightly colored alcyonarians.

D - While ending the dive, slowly being transported by the current at a depth of about 4-5 meters, it is not uncommon to see a manta ray swimming with its mouth open to take in plankton.

E - During some periods of the year, when the currents which run along the eastern side of Goidhoo nearly disappear, huge groups, sometimes in the thousands, of pelagic fish such as jacks gather in this area, perhaps in order to mate.

are two large bull sharks resting on the bottom of the large cave in the reef; if disturbed they will lazily swim away. Going back up you will find formations of great red alcyonarians and all the inhabitants of the coral reef. During the winter season it is not uncommon to encounter manta rays swimming against the current to filter out the plankton. On the top of the reef there are entire families of humphead wrasses. On more than one occasion you may see groups of them, especially near the surface. This dive must be well-planned. In addition to the usual rules to follow for drift dives, you must be very careful not to venture too far from the wall, for example to photograph the school of barracudas at the water's surface, as it becomes very difficult to turn back against the current pushing out to the open sea.

PHOTOGRAPHY

The walls of Goidhoo offer so many photo opportunities that you could make dozens of dives with different optical systems and still get excellent images. The wide-angle lens is indispensable for good shots of barracudas, who are easy to approach, and the schools of jacks, but especially for backlighting against the branches of red coral. The 28 mm is useful for taking shots of individual fish, in particular dolphins, as they never get too close to scuba divers.

F - A humpback wrasse (Cheilinus undulatus) and a clown triggerfish (Balistoides conspicullum) swim near each other in a detritic area on the upper part of the reef.

G - Even these barracudas (Sphyraena sp.), that seem to be ready to "embrace" the photographer, gather in the waters of Goidhoo, perhaps in order to mate.

ARI ATOLL

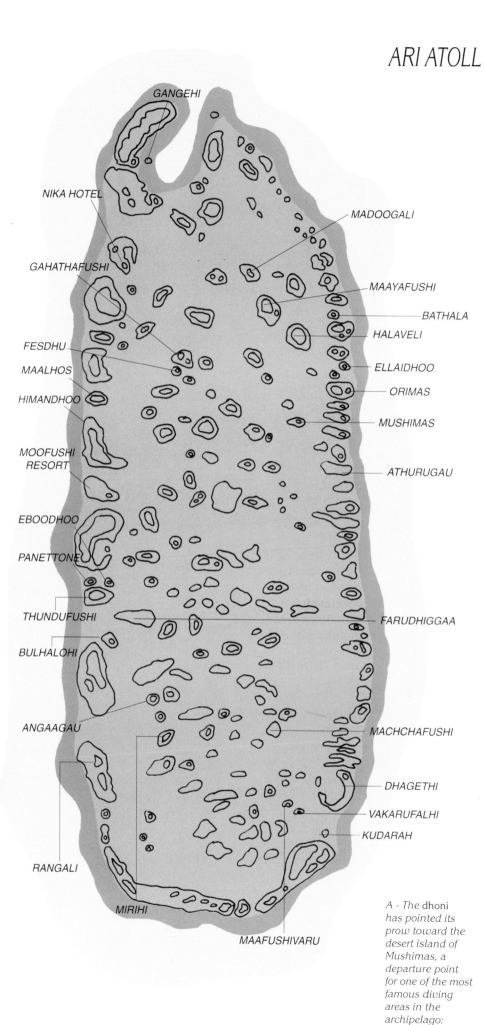

GANGEHI
NIKA HOTEL
GAHATHAFUSHI
FESDHU
MAALHOS
HIMANDHOO
MOOFUSHI RESORT
EBOODHOO
PANETTONE
THUNDUFUSHI
BULHALOHI
ANGAAGAU
RANGALI
MIRIHI
MAAFUSHIVARU

MADOOGALI
MAAYAFUSHI
BATHALA
HALAVELI
ELLAIDHOO
ORIMAS
MUSHIMAS
ATHURUGAU
FARUDHIGGAA
MACHCHAFUSHI
DHAGETHI
VAKARUFALHI
KUDARAH

A - The dhoni has pointed its prow toward the desert island of Mushimas, a departure point for one of the most famous diving areas in the archipelago: Shark Thila.

The Ari Atoll is one of the largest in the Maldivian archipelago. It extends 48 miles from east to west. Administratively the coral agglomerates of Rasdhoo and the island of Thoddoo, famous for its vegetable crops, especially watermelons, are also part of the Ari Atoll. Eighteen islands are inhabited by indigenous peoples. Population is about 11,000 people. There are about 26 resorts. The administrative capital is Mahibadhoo, on the southeast side. In addition to large fishing islands like Dhigurah, Dhangethi, Mandhoo, Feridhoo, there about 33 desert islands in the Ari Atoll that can be explored. A cruise to Ari offers some of the most famous and spectacular dives in the entire archipelago.

A

SOME RESORT IN ARI ATOLL

Gangehi has 25 tastefully furnished bungalows in local style, built on piles, some on the water. Refined atmosphere with discreet entertainment and excellent food.
Avi Resort on Velidhoo Island, 30 rooms with basic but comfortable structures.
Bathala, on the east side of the atoll, includes 38 circular cottages with various styles of interior decorating. Central European clientele.

Maayafushi, opened in 1983 with 20 rooms, then increased to 60, is very popular, especially with Germans.

Halaveli, a crescent-shaped island with a beautiful beach, has 50 rooms with a mostly Italian clientele. Rather simple and informal structure.

Ellaidhoo houses its central European clientele in 50 rooms with thatched roofs and basic furnishings. There is a soccer field on the island.

Ranveli has 56 rooms in two-story blocks of 4 and is under Italian management. Common areas have very refined wood and rattan furnishings.

Kuda Rah is under Italian management, with 30 very large bungalows (5 on the water) which are carefully furnished. There are tennis courts and a swimming pool on the island, with entertainment by Club Vacanze. Tropical garden with fruit trees.

Vakarufalhi is the quintessential tropical island, with thatched roofs on the 50 bungalows that can

D

E

B

C

barely be seen under the palms, surrounded by a shining white beach. The resort is relatively new.

Ari Beach is an informal village with 85 chalets on the long beach. Popular with the English and Germans.

Machchafushi opened in 1993, has 60 luxuriously finished rooms hidden in a thick palm grove.

Maafushivaru is also known as Twin Island, because there is a similar island nearby where the Hummingbird helicopter that transports visitors from the airport to the village lands. Opened in 1990, it has 38 bungalows with unusual blue roofs, very well-cared for facilities and discreet entertainment. Italian clientele.

Rangali is the most westerly village in the archipelago, with 100 simple yet functional rooms built on the beach. It has a cosy atmosphere.

Mirihi is a small circular island with 34 lodges.

Angaagau is a tranquil, well-cared for facility with Maldivian-European furnishings and a very

A - From the cabin of the **Hummingbird** *one can enjoy a breathtaking view; a helicopter ride is certainly one of the best ways to observe the conformation of the atolls.*

B - Kuda Rah is on the far south end of the Ari Atoll. It is a coral island covered with lush vegetation where an excellent resort is located.

C - A large white beach completely surrounds the Island of Halaveli, where the village of the same name is located.

D - Ranveli, a small resort, is a little tongue of sand between the ocean and the splendid lagoon protected by the coral reef.

E - Sea turtles come to deposit their eggs on deserted beaches like this one, laboriously dragging themselves across the sand for what may be dozens of meters.

F - This areal view shows the resort of Thundufushi. Thick vegetation grows everywhere, concealing and shading the elegantly furnished bungalows.

B

young clientele.

Thundufushi has 42 well-furnished bungalows in Italian style, with simple verandahs on the beach. Frequented by Italians and the English.

Athurugau has the same facilities as Thundufushi and same level of comfort, as the resorts were built by the same company, which still manages them. Italian and German clientele.

Moofushi, on the western edge of the atoll, has 60 rooms (some on piles in the water). It was opened in 1990. Mostly Italian clientele.

Fesdhu has 50 bungalows, which were renovated in 1995 and are surrounded by bougainvillea bushes; the nearby island of **Gahathafushi** is very beautiful, and couples who want to relive the atmosphere of Blue Lagoon can arrange to be left on this desert island from dawn until dusk, with water and food provided.

Madoogali Resort, with 50 rooms located in the middle of a botanical garden, where some of the plants grow only here, is under Italian management. Friendly atmosphere and excellent service.

Nika Hotel has 24 carefully furnished, circular cottages with very refined architecture.

HUMMINGBIRD HELICOPTERS

The different styles of the over 70 resorts on the Maldives make it possible for everyone to find the style that best suits their needs. In the past, the relative distance from the tourist villages to the airport created many problems for resort visitors, who had to make long, inconvenient transfers on slow boats; today, almost all operators utilize a very comfortable and fast transfer service, the *Hummingbird* helicopters. This transport company has been operating in the Maldives since 1989, and during the peak season its helicopters, which seat 22 persons each, transport 5,000 passengers a month from Hulule, where the airport is located, to heliports scattered throughout the atolls

near the villages.
A helicopter ride over the archipelago is certainly an unforgettable experience; the panorama that greets your eyes as you gaze down from above is truly unique. It is also possible to organize normal excursions in *Hummingbird* helicopters, as well as "photo flights."

C

D

E

F

ORIMAS THILA

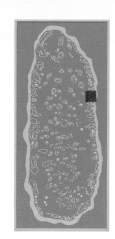

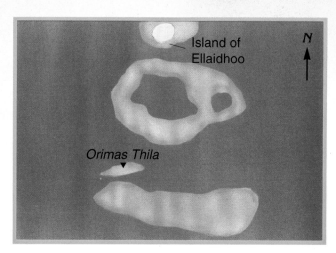

Island of
Ellaidhoo

Orimas Thila

N

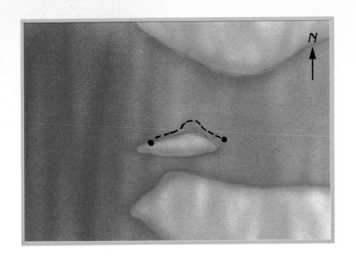

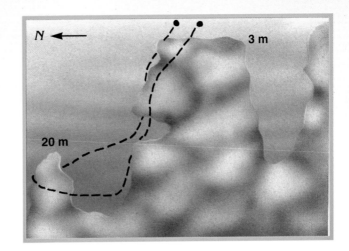

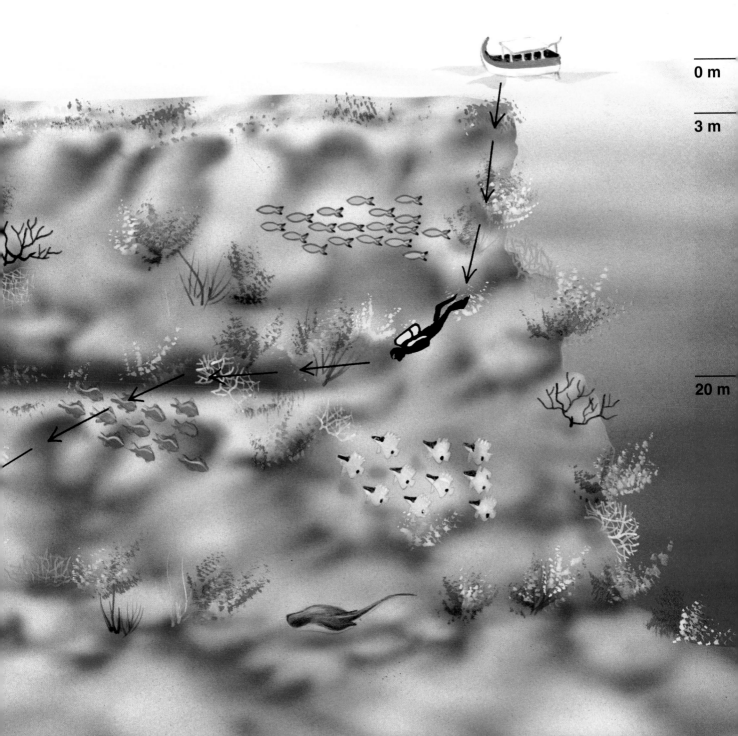

A

B

A - *Hundreds of yellowtail fairy basslets* (Pdeudanthias evansi) *swim over formations of* Acropora *coral; the small fish take refuge among the tangled corals when they sense danger.*

B - *Like a swarm of insects, this cloud of glassfish darts rapidly before the photographer.*

C - *Red whip corals grow sparsely on the more exposed areas of the reef.*

D - *These bushes of* Ellisella *grow toward the sun like flames.*

LOCATION

The thila is in the eastern part of the Ari Atoll, to be precise between the emerging reefs (called in Maldivian *faru*) of Orimas and Maagau. Nearby islands are Ellaidhoo, a tourist island, and Konagau, a small desert island. The diving area is a shoal that rises from a sandy bottom about 30 meters deep to 2-3 meters from the surface. The southern side of the coral block is very close to the *faru* of Orimas, which joins it to form a sort of canyon. Deep cracks open up on the northern side, along with a small grotto. There is a coral mushroom 10 meters in diameter a little distance from the shoal.

DESCRIPTION OF THE DIVE

The best side to explore is beyond doubt the side facing north.
The entry point depends on the current; when incoming, it will be on the east point, while you should enter on the opposite side when the current is flowing out of the atoll. Most of your time on the floor will

C

D

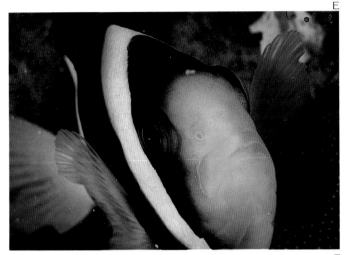

be spent exploring the grotto and the surrounding area, with a safety stop at a depth of 5 meters on the top reef after you have sent the signal buoy to the surface.

The entire reef is covered with many large hard coral formations *(Montipora)* that offer shelter to a multitude of brightly colored reef fish. At the entry to the deep crack in the wall of the shoal is a dense school of bigeye emperors *(Monotaxis grandoculis)*, which float motionless with their snouts against the current. In the grotto you will find the usual inhabitants of the most sheltered areas of the reef: red soldierfish and red and silver bigeyes that come out into the open water only at night to feed on shrimp and small crabs.

In the sandy pass on the floor of the channel one encounters the rare feathertail stingray *(Hypolophus sephen)*. This stingray is identifiable by its yellow coloring and the "plume" on the end of its tail. Although Orimas Thila is close to two tourist villages, its reef is colorful and full of life.

E - A small Clark's anemonefish (Amphiprion clarkii) advances menacingly toward the photographer's lens.

F - In the shallower portion of the giri there are splendid coral formations such as these large umbrellas of Acropora.

G - A trumpetfish (Aulostomus chinensis) in its characteristic vertical position hovers over an intricate formation of sponges.

H - The coral garden at Orimas is incredibly luxuriant. This group of soldierfish (Myripristis vittata) swims among thick sea-fans and numerous crinoids.

You should respect this little ecosystem by being careful not to step on even the sandy bottom of the grotto in order to avoid upsetting the delicate balance of the coral reef.

PHOTOGRAPHY

For those who prefer seascapes, Orimas Thila offers shots for any focal length. Using a wide-angle lens, you can approach the school of bigeye emperors for a frontal shot, perhaps with a scuba diver in the background. Be careful to use the flash sparingly, as the silvery scales of the fish reflect a great deal of light. Using a 28 mm or 35 mm, the small

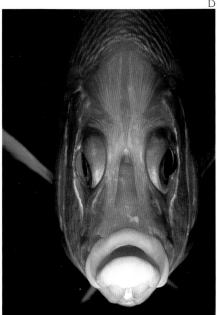

groups of soldierfish will be excellent subjects for a photo in warm red tones. If you come across any stingrays, never approach them near the tail: to get good shots, come close from below, facing them and keeping your eye on the viewfinder ready to snap the picture.

A - A solitary snapper (Lutjanus monostigma) *has infiltrated a school of unicornfish* (Naso hexacanthus).

B - The dwarf yellow-spotted goby (Eviota sebreei) *lives camouflaged on the seabed.*

C - Two lizardfish (Synodus jaculum) remain motionless among the corals waiting for fish to fall into their ambush.

D - The squirrelfish is quite territorial and will attack anyone who invades its area.

E - Another predator that uses camouflage techniques to ambush its prey is the longnose hawkfish (Oxycirrhitus typus).

F - At the approach of a diver, this grouper (Anyperodon leucogrammicus) takes refuge in a cavity among the Goniopora.

G - These red-tailed butterflyfish (Chaetodon collare) live sheltered under an umbrella-shaped coral formation.

H - Several large alcyonarians grow from the vertical wall, creating pleasing patches of color.

I - A coral grouper (Cephalopholis miniata) fearlessly approaches the photographer's lens, giving him time to frame the shot.

FESDHOO WRECK

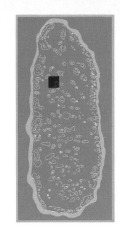

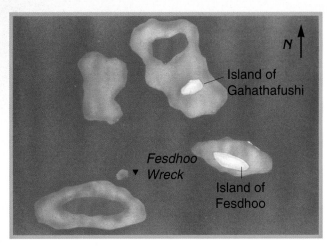

Island of
Gahathafushi

*Fesdhoo
Wreck*

Island of
Fesdhoo

N

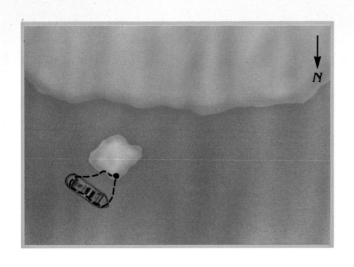

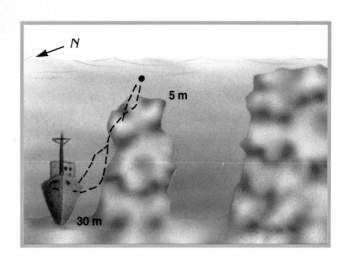

LOCATION

The *Fesdhoo wreck* is situated
in the central portion of the Ari Atoll.
It sank a few years ago, creating
a new and impressive scuba diving
area. The exact location is north of
a large circular reef, near a beautiful
coral shoal 5 meters below the
surface. The nearest island is
Fesdhoo, which has a tourist village.
The wreck lies on a sandy seabed
30 meters deep, in navigating
position, and the first metallic
structures can be found 20 meters
below the surface.

DESCRIPTION OF THE DIVE

This is an incredibly varied dive
that allows you to explore a wreck,
swim around a *thila* and continue
along the reef wall to the surface.
Start by diving directly onto the ship,
and after examining the outside,
go to the bridge and enter what was
once the cabin. Leaving the wreck,
you reach the small shoal about
10 meters away, and after
examining all its recesses, go to the

C

A

B

reef and surface slowly.
Although the most exciting part
of this dive is the overall view of
the wreck, don't forget that the coral
polyps have created a real garden
of the bare wreckage, covering
it with colorful encrustations and soft
corals. Parrotfish swim around the
wreckage, always intent on biting
at the hard calcareous bases of the
coral, and there are also butterflyfish
and red coral groupers. The heads
of large morays pop out of some
of the holes, and near the stern is
a large school of batfish.
Schools of jacks often pass by.
Another resident in the area is
a humphead wrasse which never
goes too close to divers. Inside the
cabin is a compact wall of glassfish
and several white alcyonarians.
The sandy bottom around the wreck
is an ideal habitat for stingrays and
small blackspotted gardeneels
(Heteroconger hassi). Formations
of glassfish swim on the *thila*.
Crossing a narrow channel, you
come to the vertical wall of the reef,
where you may encounter triggerfish,
large numbers of angelfish and all
the small inhabitants of the reef.

E - A sociable humpback wrasse (Cheilinus undulatus) *follows divers during their visit.*

F - Hundreds of small Indian flame blassets (Pseudanthias ignitus) *swim near the propeller, where white alcyonarians and a small bush of black coral have grown.*

G - The walls of the ship have been entirely encrusted by the red-orange cups of Tubastrea, *a coral which prefers sheltered and dimly lit areas.*

Looking out toward the open sea, you may sometimes see eagle rays passing by. As the interior of the wreck is rather cramped, only expert divers with a good source of illumination should attempt it. Be careful of the metallic structures, which can cause painful injuries. Although it is artificial, the wreck should be considered as alive as the reef. You should therefore avoid leaning on the metallic structures and must maintain a perfect position to avoid destroying years of work.

PHOTOGRAPHY

Using a super wide-angle lens, you can catch the entire wreck in these crystal clear waters. An image of the prow with a diver in the background is quite impressive. Use the flash sparingly when you photograph the dense school of glassfish.

F

D

E

G

EMMAS THILA

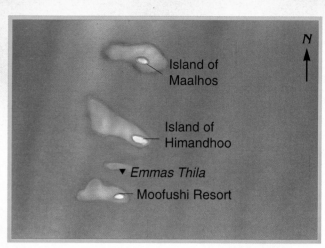

Island of Maalhos

Island of Himandhoo

▼ *Emmas Thila*

Moofushi Resort

N

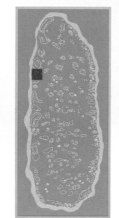

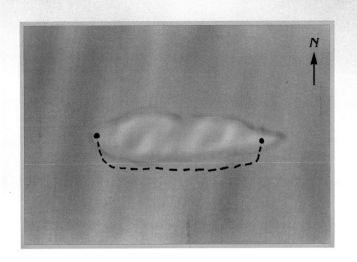

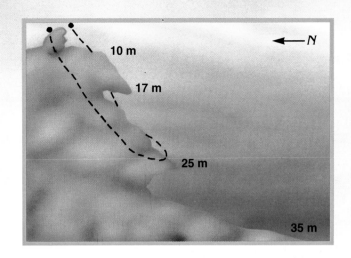

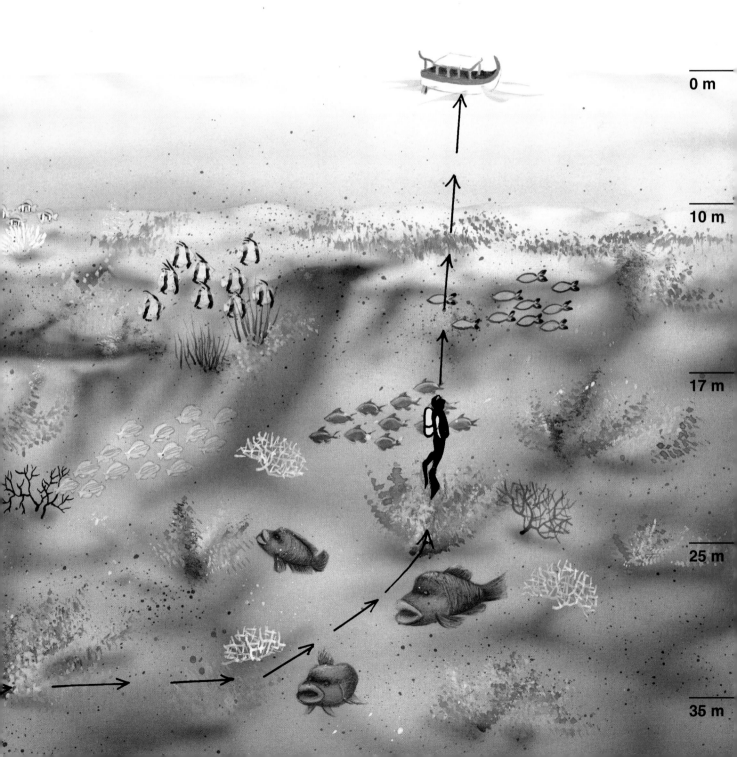

LOCATION

The Emmas Thila is located in the Ari Atoll, with nearby islands that include Himandhoo to the north, with a typical Maldivian village, and the Moofushi tourist island to the south. The diving area is a reef that rises from a seabed about 35 meters deep, with almost vertical walls, to 10 meters from the surface. The coral base has an elongated form that runs from east to west and is situated in the middle of an oceanic channel. Its southern side is broken by horizontal cracks.

DESCRIPTION OF THE DIVE

During the winter months, when the predominant currents are flowing out of the atoll, the dive begins on the southeast side of the *thila*. At this point, when you reach a depth of 15-17 meters, you will find a deep crack in the wall: after exploring this grotto, descend to the bottom, where you will find another recess in the reef at a depth of about 27 meters.

When your air reserves and remaining down-time require you to surface, if the current permits try to swim almost vertically, as the reef is not very long. In any event, you must make a safety stop in open water attached to the signal balloon. In Dhivehi, the Maldivian language, *emmadi* means manta ray, and in fact this is one of the best areas for observing these fascinating creatures. They are usually encountered at fairly shallow depths, about 10-15 meters, often with a remora, or sharksucker, attached to their backs, providing a thrilling sight as they majestically glide by. Sometimes, when sailing to the diving area, you may even see one jump from the water and land on its back. However, manta rays are not the only attraction of this area: dense bunches of alcyonarians grow on the walls of the reef, surrounded by schools of anthias and other small fish. There are often large humphead wrasses that rotate curiously, always keeping an eye on the divers. At the base of the mass there are certain areas with numerous red whip corals. Compact groups of young bannerfish

E - Humpback wrasses (Cheilinus undulatus) *can reach over two meters in length and hundreds of kilos in weight. Adults can be recognized by a clear frontal swelling.*

F - Groups of sweetlips (Plectorhinchus orientalis) *and butterflyfish* (Chaetodon collare) *gather on the top of the reef.*

G - There are several deep horizontal cracks at the base of the shallow where large gray sharks often rest.

(Heniocus sp.) swim around these corals. As the reef is located near the open sea, you may even encounter gray sharks and whitetip sharks. This dive is for experienced divers only, as during certain periods of the year the currents can be quite powerful. In this case you may need to cancel the dive and move to a more sheltered area.

PHOTOGRAPHY

The manta rays are certainly the most sought-after images in this dive. For good results you need to follow a few rules: always swim under or at the most at the same depth as the manta rays, never try to follow them, and don't stop at coral formations or pinnacles which are detached from the seabed: these are usually grooming stations, and the manta rays leave when they see that they are occupied by another animal. Depending on how close you think you can get to the subject, choose a 15 to 20 millimeter lens. Your flash should always be at low power.

D

F

G

PANETTONE

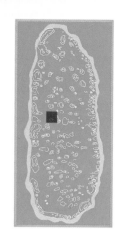

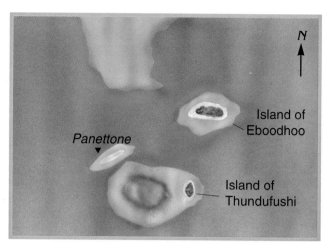

Island of
Eboodhoo

Panettone

Island of
Thundufushi

N

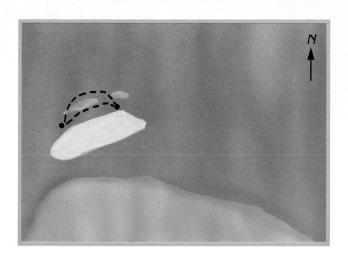

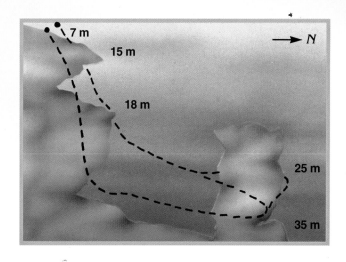

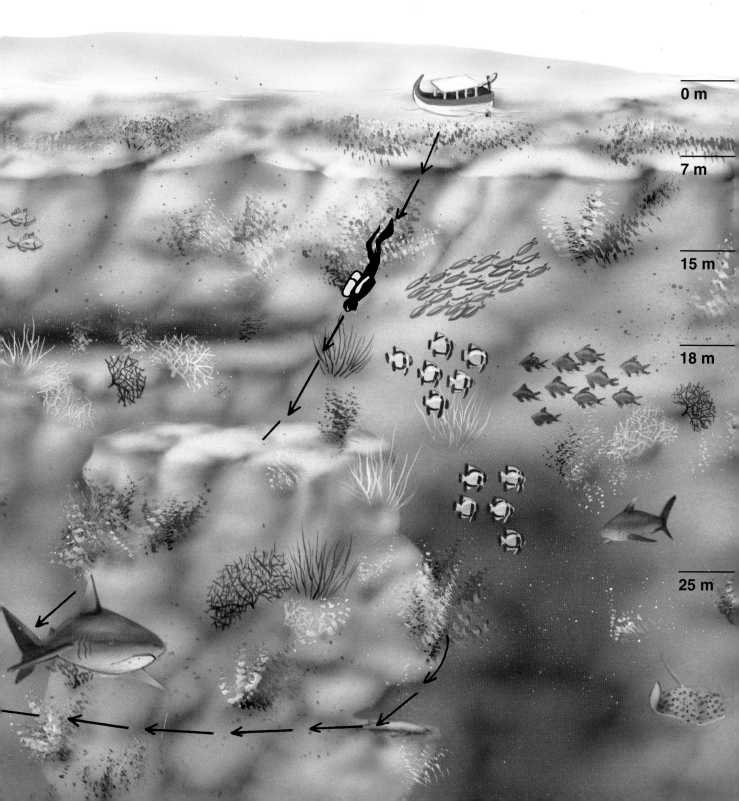

0 m

7 m

15 m

18 m

25 m

7 m

15 m

18 m

25 m

35 m

N

N

A - During a dive on Panettone one can admire marvelous formations of yellow alcyonarians which grow on the vertical walls of the reef.

B - The mantas approach the reef only when they want to avail themselves of the services of cleaner fish in order to rid themselves of parasites; otherwise they stay in the deep sea and follow plankton migrations.

C - The form of a diver can be glimpsed among the delicate fronds of a large sea-fan to which several crinoids are attached.

D - With their vivid and brilliant red color, some long sea whips enlight the vertical walls of Panettone.

LOCATION

The so-called Panettone is on the western edge of the central part of the Ari Atoll, in the middle of an oceanic pass. Neighboring islands are Thundufushi, where there is a tourist village, and Eboodhoo, which is uninhabited. This is an elongated coral formation which extends from a depth of 35 meters to the surface, with vertical walls broken by numerous grottos and crevices. The portion which emerges at the surface is easily recognizable because it forms a little hill of sand. On the northern side of the formation, more or less in the center, there are two large isolated coral mushrooms that rise from the sandy bottom to 18 meters from the surface.

DESCRIPTION OF THE DIVE

Panettone's southern side is the most interesting, so the dive should begin here, depending on the current, which always governs dives in channels. Enter the water from one of the two peaks of the shoal and descend along the wall.
At depths of 15 and 25 meters, you will want to explore two large cracks which are particularly interesting and full of life.
Once you reach the large isolated formation, your decision to go around it from the outside or stay near the wall will depend the strength of the current. Following the outline of the seabed, you will come to a sheltered area, where

you can easily ascend to the surface in contact with the reef. This is one of the most exciting dives in the entire atoll.
The interesting play of currents that carry in nourishment has encouraged the growth of whip corals, sea fans and a multitude of brightly colored soft corals. Dense schools of bannerfish, yellowfin fusiliers and jacks swim among the corals, along with all the other small, colorful inhabitants of the reef. As you begin to ascend from the sandy bottom, where you will see large stingrays that move with a characteristic waving motion of their broad mantles, you may see some gray sharks. A large nurse shark lives in a crevice in one of

the isolated masses, where it remains immobile even when approached. A few whitetip sharks swim near the reef.
Usually at a depth of 5 to 20 meters you may encounter the lords of Panettone: the mantas. They glide slowly and majestically, some with their mouths open, the appendages of their heads forming a funnel to convey the plankton on which they feed, while others hover at the water's surface to permit cleaner fish to free them from parasites.
The extremely professional instructors from the nearby diving school, who are quite sensitive to the protection of their diving areas, have succeeded in keeping this

reef almost completely intact. It is thus wise to leave the seabed in the same condition in which you found it, and to be sure not to touch anything.

PHOTOGRAPHY

Photographers will find enough shots here to fill quite a lot of rolls of film. A wide-angle lens is necessary for close-up photos of the mantas and the schools of small fish. Even standard lenses are sufficient for taking shots of the sharks and stingrays. Those who prefer macro photos will find extremely interesting subjects in the many crevices in the wall.

E - A diver passes under a natural arch extraordinarily embellished with a true flowering of orange alcyonarians.

F - The bright scales of this squirrelfish are nearly camouflaged among the red cups of the Tubastrea *coral and brilliant alcyonarians on the wall.*

G - The nurse shark (Nebrius ferrugineus) remains hidden in the cavities of the coral reef by day, coming out at night to hunt fish and cephalopods. Its rather flat snout is characterized by two barb-shaped sensory organs. Although it is peaceful by nature, it can become dangerous if overly disturbed.

THUNDUFUSHI THILA

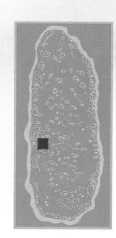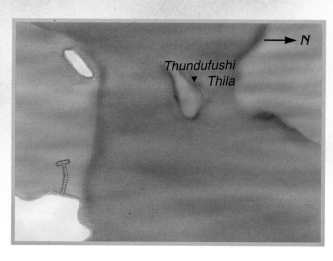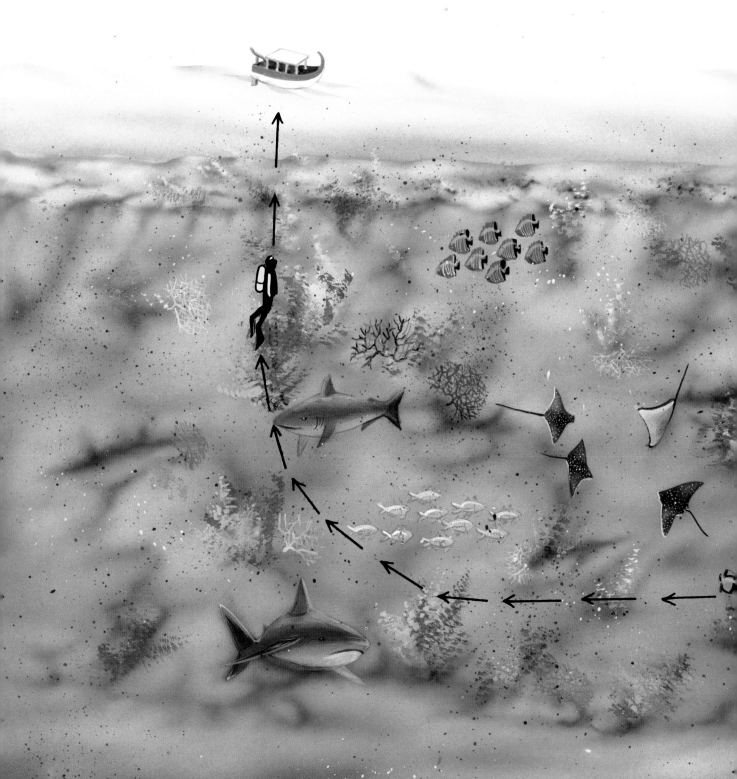

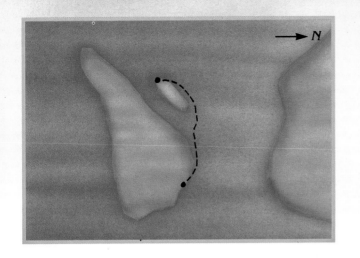

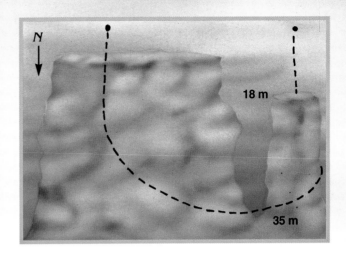

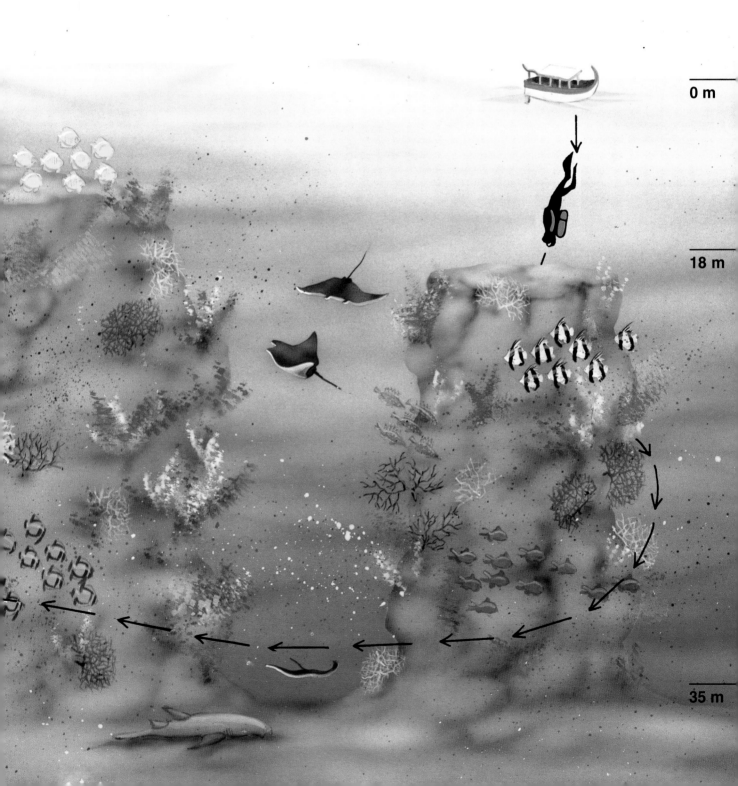

LOCATION

The *thila* of Thundufushi is situated on the western side of the Ari Atoll. The diving area is a shoal within a pass. The base of the coral platform is on a sandy seabed 35 meters deep and comes to about 12 meters from the surface. On the northern side of the *thila* is a coral block which extends from the bottom to 18 meters from the surface. The walls of the shoal are full of cracks.
The nearest island is Thundufushi, where the Maldiviana Sea Club is located.

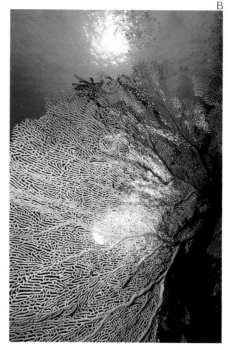

A - As he rises along the wall, a diver is approached by a silvery mass of lunar fusilierfish (Caesio lunaris) descending toward the seabed.

B - Here one can clearly see the dense branches that make up the delicate structure of a sea-fan.

C - It is always thrilling to encounter a group of eagle rays (Aetobatus narinari). Sometimes one may see more than thirty individuals passing by. These rays are ovoviviparous and give birth to 1 to 4 baby rays after a gestation period of 12 months.

D - This image documents the passage of a group of unusual jacks (Trachinotus blochii) near the water's surface; these pelagians prefer to live near the estuaries of rivers, but occasionally can be seen around the Maldives.

DESCRIPTION OF THE DIVE

This dive is for scuba divers with a medium to high level of expertise who are practiced in drift diving. Divers usually enter the water from the northwest part of the shoal, with the current flowing into the atoll. When you reach the top reef, go down along the drop and come to the desired depth, then proceed following the wall until you reach the large detached block. Once you have gone around this coral tower, begin ascending until you come to the top of the shoal, then let go for the safety stop in open water, at the same time sending up the inflatable signal buoy.

The *thila*'s position within a channel swept by currents is the reason for such an incredible variety of alcyonarians on the walls. Along with the soft corals, sea fans and sea whips, branches of black coral and other splendid coral formations adorn the reef. There are always gray sharks in this area, swimming peacefully not far from the plateau.
Looking up, you can see groups of eagle rays floating motionless in the current. In the deeper recesses of the wall, resting on the floor, are nurse sharks.
Jacks often swirl around the coral mushroom, their snouts to the current, the whole school moving in rapid jerks. The crevices in the coral mass are home to groups

of butterflyfish and compact formations of soldierfish.
The timid hawkfish moves warily among the branches of black coral, and if you look down to the seabed you will see the rhythmic ballet of the fire gobies. Be extremely careful when you move along the sides of the shoal, carried by fairly strong currents, as it is easy to damage the alcyonarians and corals that jut out from the wall. Always be very careful to check your position and your distance from the reef.

PHOTOGRAPHY

Countless seascape photos are possible here. You can use a wide-angle lens to capture the alcyonarians that enliven the wall, perhaps with a scuba diver in the blue depths in the background. Lenses such as a 28 mm or 35 mm are useful for small groups of fish or an impressive photo of the eagle rays against the light, taken from below. Macro photography is possible only when the currents are very weak, as one must stay as still as possible in order to frame the picture properly.
The 20 mm is an ideal lens for the large gray sharks that often come within range.

E - The presence of weak but constant currents along the edges of the thila *has encouraged the development of thick clusters of alcyonarians.*

F - A pair of masked bannerfish (Heniochus monoceros) circles a projection of coral.

G - The waters around Thundu thila *are often patrolled by solitary gray sharks.*

BULHAALHOHI GIRI

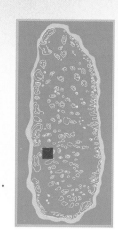

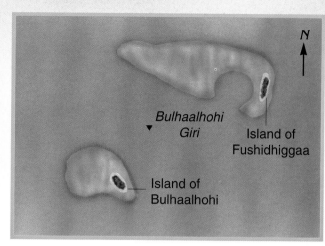

Bulhaalhohi Giri

Island of
Fushidhiggaa

Island of
Bulhaalhohi

N

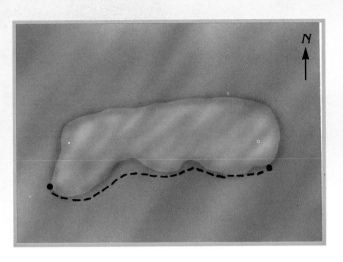

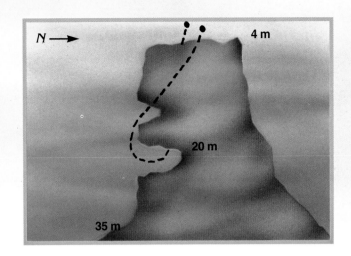

0 m

4 m

20 m

LOCATION

The Bulhaalhohi shoal is located in the southwestern part of the Ari Atoll, between the long reef of Dhiggaa and the desert island of Bulhaalhohi. The shallower part of the *giri* is about 3 meters from the surface, and its walls plunge vertically to 35 meters deep. It is about a hundred meters long, with an elongated form running from east to west.

DESCRIPTION OF THE DIVE

The coral bank is rather far within the western edge of the atoll, but as there is no reef to protect it, it is always swept by weak currents.
For better visibility, particularly in winter, it is best to dive when the current is flowing out.
Most dives begin along the southeast side. Keeping the wall to the right, at a depth of 15-20 meters you will find numerous cracks and grottos, some quite

C

A

B

deep, with coral formations that develop vertically, forming columns.
The dive ends at the western point, where you will make a safety stop at a shallow depth. As it is swept by slight but constant currents which carry food to benthonic organisms, the shoal is an explosion of life. The grottos are full of sea fans, almost always decorated by crinoids, soft corals that offer shelter to an incredible number of reef fish. At the entry to the largest grotto is a school of batfish.
As you enter the grottos, the compact walls of glassfish often open up enough to allow you to glimpse the snout of a gray shark resting on the sea floor. In fact, if you look into the blue depths you are likely to see small groups of these sharks. If you are lucky and very observant, in a little crevice in the wall at a depth of 10 meters you may see a small leaf fish *(Taenianotus traiacanthus)*.
The summit is covered with sarcophytes and sea anemones.

PHOTOGRAPHY

This is a classic dive suitable for all lenses. Use a wide-angle lens for seascape photos: photographs taken from within the grottos toward the outside with a nice red sea fan in the foreground are particularly effective. You will also get good results using intermediate lenses such as the 28 mm, very useful for photographing fish from a certain distance. This dive is a paradise for macro photography fans, especially if you have an amphibious camera, which will provide excellent photos even of subjects which are hard to approach.

E - The Bulhaalhohi grottos always hold some surprises. Sometimes dense schools of glassfish hide a resident who is better left undisturbed. When entering these grottos it is wise to take small steps as your eyes grow accustomed to the shadows, or else use a lamp; when a gray shark almost 2 meters long like this one decides to leave, being in its way could create a very unpleasant situation.

F - A bulging example of a gray shark, probably a pregnant female, rests at the bottom of a crevice after the fatigue of nighttime hunting.

G - In areas where currents are very strong, the sea-fans are denser and larger than elsewhere.

KUDA RAH THILA

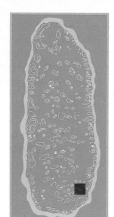

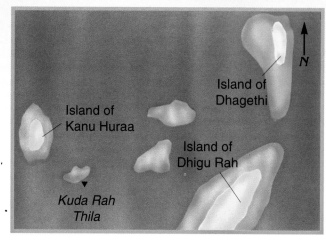

Island of
Kanu Huraa

Island of
Dhagethi

Island of
Dhigu Rah

*Kuda Rah
Thila*

N

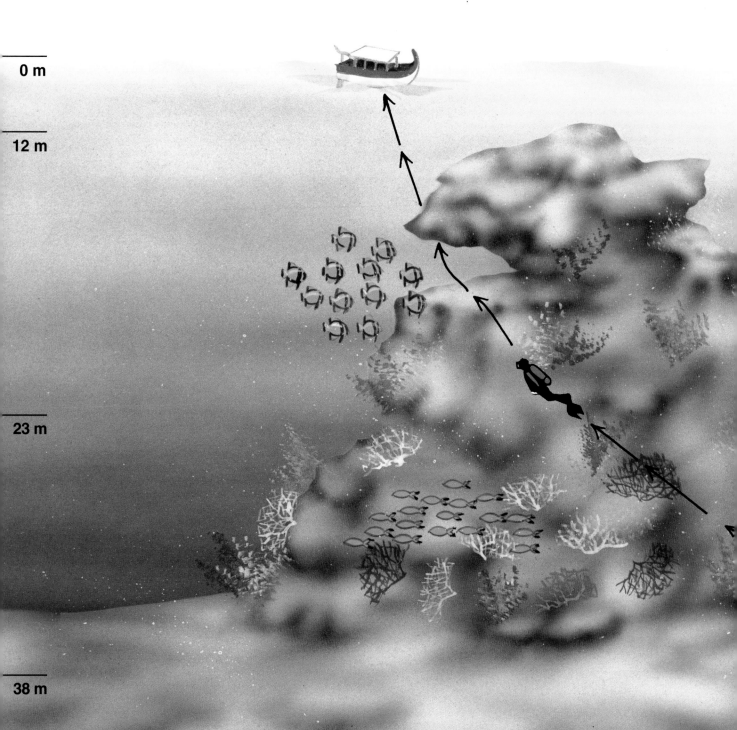

0 m

12 m

23 m

38 m

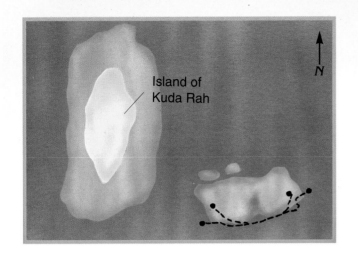

Island of
Kuda Rah

N

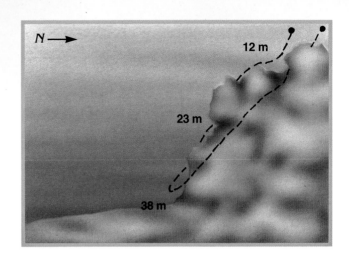

N

12 m

23 m

38 m

A - Sea-fans grow from the base of the reef at any angle that offers maximum exposure to the prevailing currents.

B - Nature creates compositions so beautiful that they leave one speechless.

C - Several red alcyonarians, perfectly illuminated in the foreground, create an excellent chromatic balance in the backlighted photo.

D - In an explosion of color, hundreds of bluestriped snappers make way as the photographer passes through.

LOCATION

The Kuda Rah Thila is in the southern part of the Ari Atoll. Nearby islands are Kuda Rah, where there is a vacation village, and Dhigu Rah, a large island inhabited by fishermen. The shoal is located at a depth of 12 to 36-38 meters from the surface and has a slightly elongated shape. One of the walls has a deep horizontal crack with an overhanging coral spur.

DESCRIPTION OF THE DIVE

Although the top of the reef is rather deep, the dive is not very complicated, and it is sufficient to enter the water at any point along the perimeter of the shoal,

C

A

D

B

descending along the walls to the desired depth and spiraling back up to explore all the crevices of the coral bed. When there is a current, you should dive in at least 20 meters from the *thila* and let yourself be carried to the point desired.

This *thila* is beyond doubt one of the most spectacular diving areas in the region. Between the top reef and the surface are schools of blue fusiliers *(Caesio lunaris)*, which often cross paths with large tunas.

The top of the shoal is embellished with thick patches of brightly-colored soft coral and the frenetic movements of the small, multi-hued inhabitants of the reef.

Near the arch is a group of snappers moving in formation, and looking off into the blue depths from this side you may easily spot some whitetip sharks as well. A school of batfish lives near the spur of rock, and quite often gathers right under it.

There are numerous sea fans on all walls of the shoal.

As powerful currents run through this area, you may have some unexpected encounters, especially with large pelagic fish.

When the currents are strong, this dive requires advanced expertise, while weak currents can be handled by divers with

any level of experience.
A scuba signal buoy for the ascent and a safety stop are indispensable.
Be very careful of the numerous sea fans which have developed on the open areas of the *thila*.
In particular when currents are strong, you should avoid grasping their fragile branches.
Be especially careful of your position when you are exploring the surface of the shoal.

PHOTOGRAPHY

Optical systems suitable for seascape photos are certainly preferable during this dive. Start from the useful 28 mm for small schools of fish and a few full frame photos of passing sharks, to the wide-angle lens for a shot from below with sea fans or an alcyonarian in the foreground and the profile of the ship silhouetted on the surface in the background.

E - A diver swims in the midst of a school of batfish (Platax teira). This species of batfish differs from other similar species due to the characteristic black spot it has on its stomach at the base of the pectoral fins.

F - A hawkfish seems perched on the branches of a tree. Hawkfish are hermaphrodites and live in harems where the male is the largest individual. When the male dies, the largest female transforms into a male.

G - Enormous groups of fusiliers gather above Kuda Rah Thila. If the current is not too powerful, there may be thousands of them.

FELIDHU ATOLL

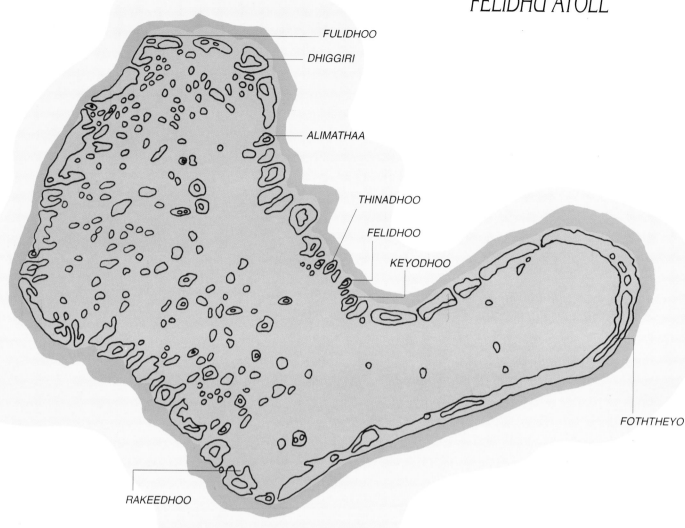

FULIDHOO
DHIGGIRI
ALIMATHAA
THINADHOO
FELIDHOO
KEYODHOO
FOTHTHEYO
RAKEEDHOO

A

B

Located between the Atolls of South Malé and Mulaku, it extends north to south for about 22 miles and from east to west for about 30 miles. Its capital, which is 42 nautical miles from Malé, is the island of Felidhoo, where the atoll is situated. With only about 1800 inhabitants, it is the Maldivian atoll with the lowest population density.

There are five islands with Maldivian villages: Fulidhoo, Thinadhoo, Felidhoo, Keyodhoo and Rakeedhoo.

The entire atoll has only two tourist resorts - **Alimathaa**, with 70 air-conditioned bungalows with hot and cold running water, a discotheque and a windsurfing and diving school, and **Dhiggiri**, with 30 air-conditioned bungalows with hot and cold running water, a discotheque and a windsurfing and diving school.

*A - The boatman
uses a rod to
measure the depth
of a small pass that
leads into the
spectacular lagoon.
Note the red cloth
on the prow of
boat; according to
popular belief, this
keeps away the evil
spirits of the sea.*

*B - Children play
joyously in the
crystal clear waters
of the lagoon of
Keyodhoo island.
The inhabitants of
the islands far from
the rush of tourists
are quite friendly.*

*C - The remains
of a lunch, once
thrown out of the
boat, attract a large
number of fish.
Cruise boats dump
only biodegradable
waste into the sea.
Plastic and other
solids are brought
back to Malé to
be incinerated.*

*D - The magnificent
underwater world
of the Maldives can
be admired in this
picture where the
thousands of colors
of the marine
creatures create
a unique spectacle.*

E

C

F

D

G

*E - This is Bodu
Mohoraa, a
mandatory stop
for cruises heading
south. This island
is truly something
close to paradise
on earth.*

*F - After the dive,
the diving* dhoni
*is moored near one
of the many desert*

*islands in the
Felidhu Atoll.
A boat holiday
makes it possible
to reach the most
pristine areas of
the archipelago.*

*G - A school of red
bigeyes brings new
colors to the blue
depth of this part of
the Indian Ocean.*

FUSHI KANDU

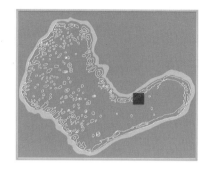

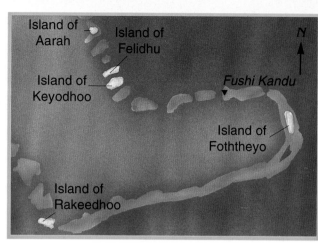

Island of Aarah
Island of Felidhu
Island of Keyodhoo
Fushi Kandu
N
Island of Foththeyo
Island of Rakeedhoo

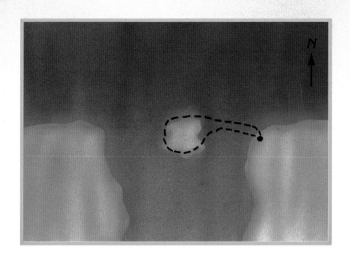

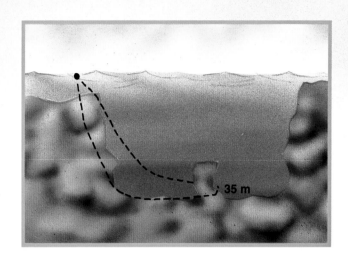

0 m

35 m

A - On the drop-off at the deepest part of the pass, one may encounter large stingrays intent on dredging the detritic floor in search of crabs and mollusks, the basis of their diet.

B - Gray sharks are a constant presence at the entry to the kandu; *large numbers of them cross the blue depths, especially when the current entering the atoll is strong.*

LOCATION

Fushi Kandu is situated in the portion of the Felidhu Atoll that stretches out towards the east. This is a rather narrow pass. The portion facing the open sea forms a broad terrace, in the center of which is a large coral mass about 5 meters high. On the oceanic side, the walls of the *kandu* drop to a depth of 35 meters. The closest islands are Foththeyo, where there is only a coconut palm plantation, and Keyodhoo, inhabited by Maldivian fishermen.

DESCRIPTION OF THE DIVE

In order to enjoy this dive to its fullest, you should enter the water with a weak incoming current. In this manner, after descending along the outside wall of the atoll to a depth of about 30 meters, you can move along the terrace to the center of the channel and explore around the coral tower that stands on its outer boundary.

C

D

A

B

Then return to the mouth of the pass and decide whether to enter the channel along the right or the left side. In any event, scuba divers will surface near the partially submerged reef. During this dive you will encounter the classic marine fauna that crosses passes less frequently by divers. In fact, given the distance from the closest diving center, only a few cruise boats ply these waters. At the mouth of the channel, where gray sharks congregate, you may encounter groups of eagle rays that hover suspended about 10 meters from the seabed. Crossing the detritic plateau that leads to the actual drop-off, you can see large stingrays out in the open, where they can be easily approached. Several sweetlips *(Plectorhinchus sp.)*, and often dense schools of fusiliers swim slowly around the coral mushroom. Looking out to the open sea, you may see large tunas and jacks which gather in this area,

C - The end of a dive is often enlivened by the high-speed passage of thousands of neon fusiliers (Pterocaesio tile), who owe their name to their particularly bright scales.

D - Usually large schools of eagle rays glide elegantly through the deep sea during daytime hours. In the late afternoon they reach the detritic floors to feed by sucking up worms and crustaceans with their mouths extended like a proboscis.

especially when the current is coming in.

When the currents are running strongly, it is wise to avoid trying to reach the coral tower about twenty meters from the mouth of the pass, as you may exhaust yourself swimming against the current.

Under normal conditions, if the crew of the *dhoni* agrees, you may cross the pass and end the dive along the outside wall of the atoll. In this case, always check surface water conditions first so that getting back on the boat is not a problem.

PHOTOGRAPHY

Photographers can use all optical systems at their disposal for this dive. Using a wide-angle lens such as a 15 millimeter, try to photograph a stingray resting on the bottom in the foreground, with a group of divers in the background. Or else take a photo of a group of sweetlips, with branches of black coral in the background.

Using standard lenses such as. the 28 or 35 millimeter, you can take impressive pictures of the group of eagle rays, with their black silhouettes outlined against the sun.

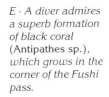

E - A diver admires a superb formation of black coral (Antipathes sp.), which grows in the corner of the Fushi pass.

F - The model, who clearly is an · expert in position techniques, hovers over a rare sea-fan

and moves a servo-flash toward the camera.

G - The form of a diving dhoni *is silhouetted on the surface; the waters in the Felidhu pass are crystal clear and visibility is over 50 meters deep.*

H - Groups of oriental sweetlips (Plectorhinchus orientalis) gather in the crevices of the internal channel; they are unmistakable with their curious striped and spotted scales.

I - A pair of clown triggerfish (Balistoides conspicillum) chase each other in the open water, perhaps during the mating season.

CIPPO THILA

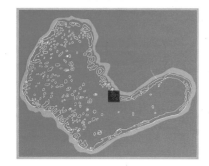

Island of
Felidhu

Island of
Keyodhoo

Cippo Thila

N

0 m

25 m

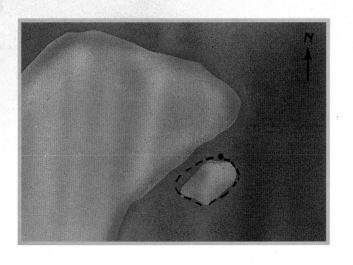

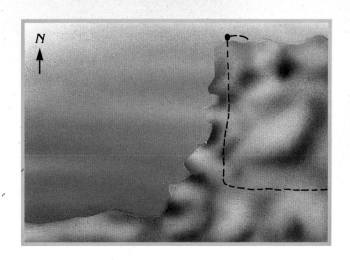

A -Various types of sea-fans grow close together at the base of the reef.

B - This image is testimony to the variety of bright colors in alcyonarians.

C - Moving cautiously, one can approach red-tailed butterflyfish (Chaetodon collare) almost close enough to touch them; these fish can thus be observed in the greatest detail.

D - This rare image shows three batfish (Platax teira) with their spectacular youthful colors. As they mature, their long fins grow shorter and give the fish its characteristic round form.

E - The "flowering" branches of a sea-fan set the backdrop for a pair of damselfish who pose to the delight of the photographer.

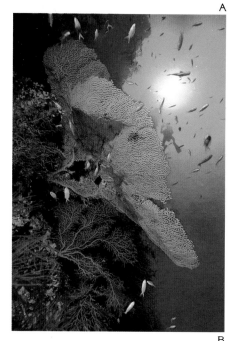

LOCATION

Cippo Thila is situated in the east central area of the Felidhu Atoll. The nearest island is Keyodhoo, where there is a Maldivian village. The shoal, located in the interior of a rather large pass, comes almost to the surface from a platform 25 meters deep. The shoal is circular in form, and on the wall facing the south there is a deep vertical crack.

DESCRIPTION OF THE DIVE

This is a very easy dive that can be done at night as well. In fact, during the evening you can see forms of life which are hidden during the day. The *thila* is rather sheltered from

currents, so it is possible to circumnavigate it completely. Begin the dive by going to the base of the shoal, and then spiral up, so that you can examine all the fissures in the walls. On the top of the reef is a spur of dead coral to which the divemaster can tie the diving *dhoni*'s mooring line, using it to mark the spot where divers will surface to get back on board the boat. This is a very colorful dive. At the base of the coral towers on the western side are sea fans and some black coral formations. Inside the vertical crack grow red-orange alcyonarians which look like bouquets of flowers when they filter the water with their polyps turned outward. Parrotfish dart frenetically all around the reef, biting at it as they feed on the algae. Numerous coral groupers *(Cephalopholis miniata)* live in the fissures, often in the company of cleaner shrimp. One peculiarity of the place is the numerous large boxfish *(Ostracion cubicus),* timid creatures which seek shelter under the jutting ledges of the wall. They are nevertheless easy to see as they move with a quick whirling of their pectoral fins. In a single evening dive you may encounter up to 20 individuals, often in pairs, in the shallower portion of the reef. Near the surface area of the *thila* there are groups of large anemones, with black-footed clownfish *(Amphiprion nigripes)* peeping out from among their tentacles. There are no special safety rules to follow in this dive.

Before entering the water you should check the strength of the current; it should permit an easy circumnavigation of the entire coral mass. As this area is rarely frequented by divers, the seabed is especially full of life. Thus, be careful not to lean on anything which may at first seem to be only a rock.

PHOTOGRAPHY

Use standard lenses to take full frame photos of fish and alcyonarians. In any case, if you have the choice, it's best to enter the water with macro photography equipment. Using lenses like a 60 or 105 mm in an underwater case, you can take splendid close-up shots of fish.

G

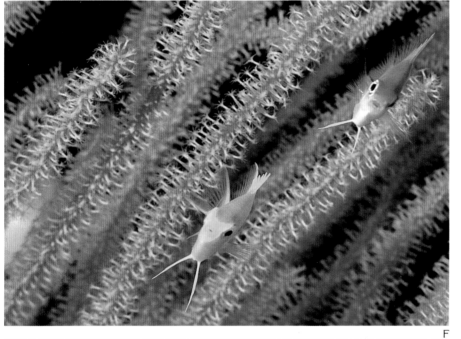
E

H

F

F - Two coral groupers (Cephalopholis minista) turn their backs to the photographer as they prepare to take refuge in a dark crevice of the reef.

G - The tentacles of the anemones contain hundred of stinging cells known as nematocysts, which are used to capture and eat
small animals as well as to keep away predators such as butterflyfish. Clownfish can live among the anemone's tentacles without problems, because their thick skin is impervious to the nematocysts.

H - The sun illuminates and brightens this small wall, which is a true coral jewel.

127

HULHIDHOO CAVES

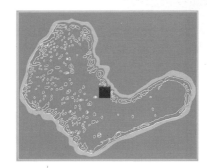

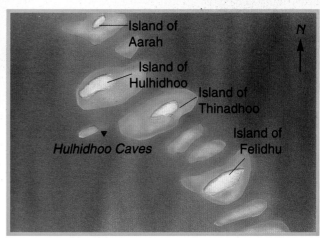

Island of Aarah

Island of Hulhidhoo

Island of Thinadhoo

Island of Felidhu

Hulhidhoo Caves

N

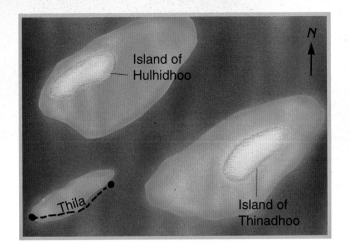

Island of Hulhidhoo

Thila

Island of Thinadhoo

N

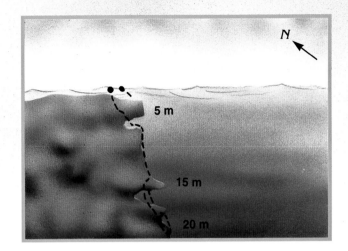

5 m

15 m

20 m

N

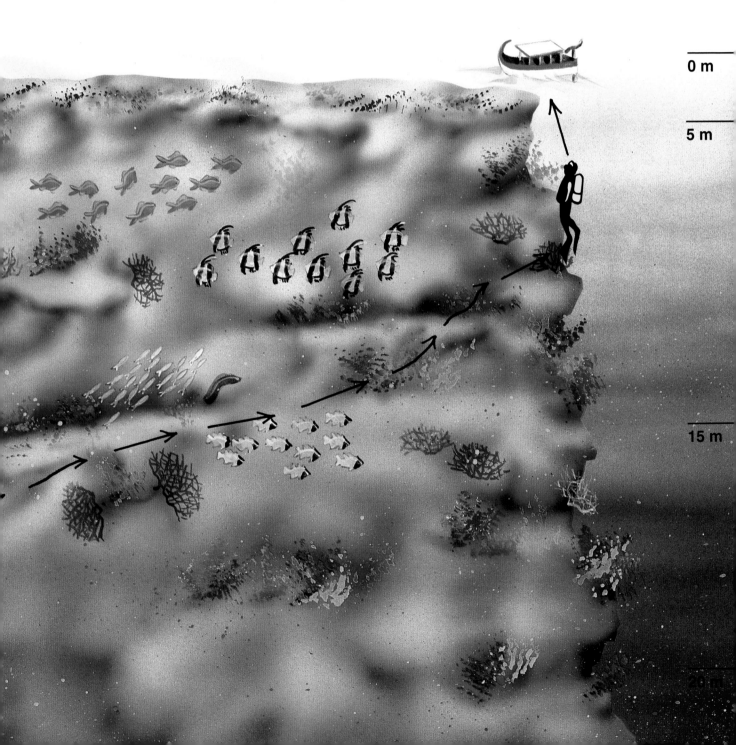

0 m

5 m

15 m

A

LOCATION

The Hulhidhoo Caves are situated in the east central portion of the Felidhu Atoll. Half of the dive is a partially submerged, elongated shoal within the pass. Nearby islands are Hulhidhoo, which is uninhabited, and Thinadhoo, with a small Maldivian village. From the surface, the reef extends down to a depth of 30 meters, and on the wall facing north there are quite beautiful grottos from 5 to 20 meters deep. The most beautiful is near the western end of the shoal, and is a two level cave with a coral column in the middle.

DESCRIPTION OF THE DIVE

The point of entry should be determined based on the strength of the current, which can sometimes be powerful. In any event, you should enter with an incoming current, about 50 meters east of the reef, to give slower divers the opportunity to descend to the desired depth.

A - Various groupers have camouflage colors that make them almost invisible when they lie in ambush. Others, like this Plectropomus areolatus, have colors that are hard not to notice.

B - The crevices of the wall are home to many leaf fish. To find them one must inspect the floor inch by inch, watching for the slightest movement.

C - This damselfish has its mouth open as it feeds on microscopic particles of zooplankton.

D - When the current is not running at Hulhidhoo, one may encounter a turkeyfish (Pterois volitans) improvising a ballet in the open water.

E - It is common to see the leopard moray (Gymnothorax undulatus) as it slithers along the rough floor.

B

C

D

A - Black coral is characteristic of the Hulhidhoo area, which is one of the most interesting diving areas in the atoll due to the large numbers and variety of its fauna.

B - Squirrelfish and soldierfish coexist peacefully during the day in the little grottos of the reef. Both species have nighttime feeding habits.

Continue to explore the cracks, staying at a depth of 20 meters, as the seabed is not particularly interesting.

The dive ends on the reef in the lee of its emerging portion. The recesses of the wall are densely populated by colorful reef fish that are well protected from the current here.

There are dense schools of glassfish in such constant movement that they appear to be a single mass that ripples and darts away when a large grouper gets too close.

All types of morays peer out of their dens. In particular, a leopard moray (Gymnothorax favagineus), which can be stroked like a cat, lives beneath a coral mushroom at a depth of about 20 meters. Semi-hidden within the protuberances, the turkeyfish puff up their "crowns of plumes" in a defensive position.

The ceilings of the grottos are thickly decorated by bunches of red and pink alcyonarians. There are also small but brilliantly

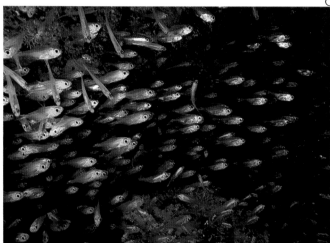

colored red-orange sea fans. From the outside corner of the reef extend branches of black coral around which swim numerous gray-green chromis. Lucky divers with a sharp eye may also see a curious leaf fish taking shelter in a small recess. Trusting its excellent camouflage, it will remain immobile even if approached.

When entering the small grottos, be careful not to lean on anything. Be certain that your position is neutral and always check the

C - Glassfish, which spend the day gathered in dark grottos, also come out at night, when they swim along the reef in search of zooplankton.

D - In its characteristic ambush position, an immobile scorpionfish patiently waits for prey to approach.

E - Oriental sweetlips (Plectorhinchus orientalis) are much more common during dives on the reefs within the atoll.

F - This lizardfish uses its camouflage abilities to best advantage as it rests on a spiny coral formation.

G - The shallower portion of the reef is a true coral garden, where thousands of tiny blue-green chromis (Chromis viridis) swim among the tangled corals.

H - Bizarre formations of soft corals can be seen along the wall. A very large sea-fan and alcyonarian happened to grow on the same rocky protuberance.

placement of your fins. Part of the reason this ecosystem maintains its balance is that it is some distance from the nearest tourist village and is consequently visited by very few divers.

PHOTOGRAPHY

This is a very colorful place which is suitable for seascape photos. The alcyonarians, with the little fish that swim near them, can be shot using standard lenses from 35 to 28 millimeters. If no portions of the sea appear in the frame, you can change the camera and flash to TTL mode. In order to photograph from the interior of the grottos toward the outside, it is better to use natural lighting so that the background will be the right shade of blue.

In order to get good macro images of the leaf fish, use a micro lens in an underwater case to avoid frightening the fish with the finder rods.

F

G

E

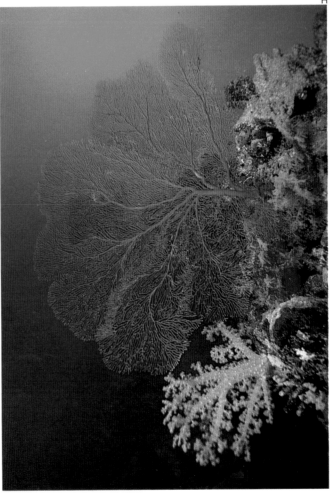

H

DHEWANA KANDU

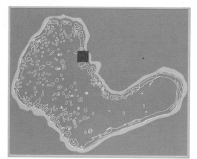

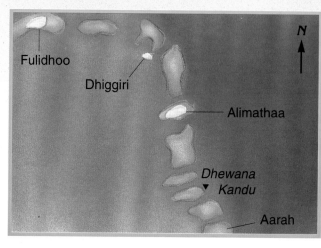

Fulidhoo

Dhiggiri

Alimathaa

Dhewana Kandu

Aarah

N

0 m

9 m

20 m

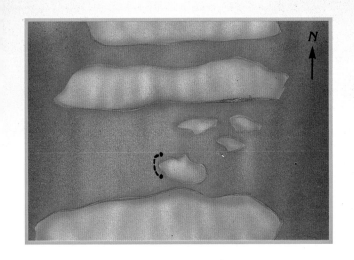

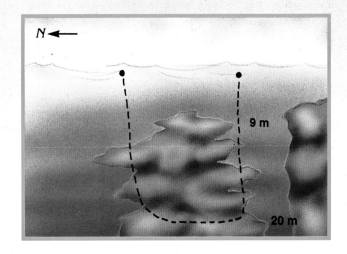

A - Multicolored formations of alcyonarians decorate the walls of the reef, while life on the coral reef goes on endlessly.

B - Large schools of bannerfish (Heniochus diphreutes) are a constant presence around the coral mushrooms of Dhewana Kandu.

C - This splendid scalefin anthias (Pseudanthias squamipinnis) was photographed during its sexual transformation from a female to a male. It still has the classic orange color of a female, but has already developed a long dorsal spine and violet spot on its pectorals, clear characteristics of a male.

D - A cascade of glassfish arrives from above, their reflections embellishing this part of the reef, on which walls grow delicate pink alcyonarians.

LOCATION

Dhewana Kandu is situated on the eastern side of the Felidhu Atoll, on its outside border. Nearby islands include Alimathaa to the north, where there is a resort, and small Aarah to the south, a magnificent desert island. This is a classic oceanic channel which contains a coral mushroom that extends from a depth of 20 meters to 9 meters from the surface. The coral structure, with terraces that form grottos and recesses, is frequented by a myriad of reef fish. Along the wall facing the pass there are three more smaller "mushrooms" with the same features.

DESCRIPTION OF THE DIVE

You should begin the dive in the open sea at the southern corner of the pass. Once you descend to the bottom of the channel, at a depth of about 28 meters, go toward the mushroom formation, where you will spend most of your time. Once you explore all the openings in the coral formation, if the current is weak you can cross the pass and end the dive near the other three "mushrooms." You will surface near the emerging reef. The Dhewana mushroom is famous for the great number of fish that live in such a restricted space. Large schools of bannerfish with white and black stripes and long dorsal fins *(Heniochus diphreutes)* gather around the terrace formations, along with numerous Moorish idols *(Zanclus cornutus).* You will find Oriental sweetlips *(Plectorhinchus orientalis),* blotcheye soldierfish *(Myripristis murdjan)* and a few morays within the recesses. Some fissures are completely decorated by thick red-orange alcyonarians, with anthias swimming among them. If you explore the floors of some of the cracks you will also find lobsters with long, constantly waving antennae, and sometimes, in the larger grottos, a few nurse sharks. You may see some

E

E - *At first glance, sea-fans seem quite robust, yet all it takes is an inadvertent blow to one of these fans to cause irreparable damage.*

F - *With their unmistakable yellow-silver color, snappers (Lutjanus monostigma) enliven the shallower area of the reef.*

G - *A giant moray (Gymnothorax javanicus) submits to the care of a cleaner fish (Labroides dimidiatus), which patiently eliminates the parasites from its skin.*

H - *A gray reef shark (Carcharhinus amblyrhynchos) is accompanied in its incessant wanderings by a pair of rainbow runners (Elagatis bipinnulata).*

F

G

whitetip sharks on the sandy bottom of the pass.
Dhewana Kandu is an ideal diving area for scuba divers with any level of experience.
Its relative depth and the currents which are never too strong in this area make it a pleasant and entertaining dive.
You should avoid touching any part of the mushroom formations, as all portions of their walls are the result of years of construction by tiny coral polyps. The high concentration of marine life means that many scuba divers come to this area: thus respect for the environment is absolutely necessary if the reef is to remain as we found it.

PHOTOGRAPHY

Lovers of close-up photos will certainly need more than one dive in order to snap all the little inhabitants of this area.
You can get good shots of the fish using 55 and 60 millimeter lenses. Use a wide-angle lens such as a 15 or 20 millimeter for a shot of a diver in the middle of a school of bannerfish, perhaps using a servoflash.

H

MIYARU KANDU

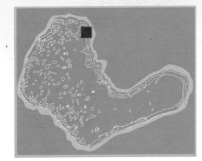

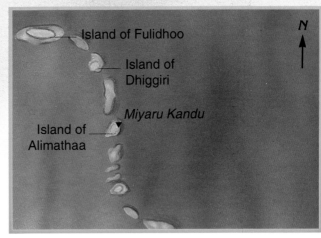

Island of Fulidhoo

Island of Dhiggiri

Miyaru Kandu

Island of Alimathaa

N

3 m

35 m

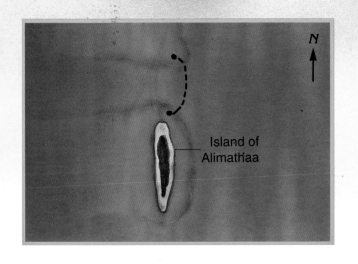

Island of
Alimathaa

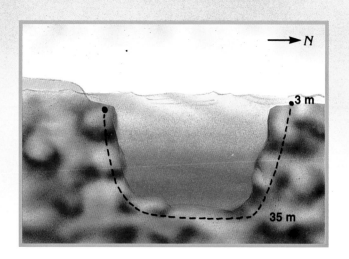

3 m

35 m

A - A group of eagle rays glides in formation off the coast of Miyaru Kandu, wings flapping in perfect synchrony.

B - The unmistakable and menacing form of a hammerhead shark (Sphyrna lewini) appears from nowhere. Usually larger individuals are solitary.

LOCATION

The dive at Miyaru Kandu is in the northeastern part of the Felidhu Atoll. It is the first pass north of the resort island of Alimathaa and is a classic drop-off in the oceanic channel.
The top of the reef, at the edges of the channel, is about 3 meters deep, then the sides plunge into the outside depths, full of little grottos and crevices.
The actual drop-off of the pass is at a depth of 33-35 meters, and the wall below is punctured by innumerable cracks rich with life, while the channel itself is rather bare due to the powerful currents that usually flow through the pass.

DESCRIPTION OF THE DIVE

The dive can be accomplished in two different ways, depending on the strength of the currents, which should always be flowing into the atoll.
When the current is strong, enter the water about 30 meters away from the reef and 50 meters north of the entry to the pass, so that you have time to descend to the desired depth without being pushed into the channel. Descend along the wall until you reach the northern corner at a depth of about 33 meters, and stop there to observe large fish passing until your down-time and air reserves force you to begin the ascent, which should be within the channel, keeping the wall to your right.
When the currents are not too powerful, you may begin the dive closer to the reef at the entry to the pass, then drift to the wall to a depth of 35 meters and cross the channel under the drop-off, ascending on the south side and finishing the dive in the atoll with the wall to your left.
In the Maldivian language, *miyaru* means shark, and these selachians are in fact always present during dives in this area. You will encounter all types of them, from whitetip sharks to gray sharks, and in the early morning you may see numerous hammerheads passing under the shelf.
Along the outside wall of the atoll, in the numerous cavities scattered throughout it, there are formations of soft corals, along with sea fans.
All types of reef fish are here. In particular, in a small grotto at a depth of about 37 meters, you may encounter two blue ribbon eels.
Near the two corners of the pass, you can see numerous eagle rays, schools of barracudas, jacks and large tunas.
As usual, dives in passes should be as close to the walls as possible. You should of course refrain from touching or leaning on them to avoid damaging the coral formations.

A

B

If the current is strong, you should not try to cross the pass, because you may be carried out to the middle of the channel and have to end your dive early.

PHOTOGRAPHY

A wide-angle lens will give you excellent photos of the school of eagle rays, as well as seascape photos of the cracks in the wall. Using 20 mm and 28 mm lenses, you can photograph the sharks, which will approach photographers as long as they do not move.
An underwater micro lens is a must for taking shots of the small, timid yellow and violet blue ribbon eels.

C

F

D

G

E

C, F - In the southern corner of the pass, strong oceanic currents carrying in nourishment have resulted in dense formations of multicolored corals.

D - Under the pass drop-off in a grotto in the wall is a small, brilliantly colored ribbon moray.

E - Gray sharks pass by in formation where the wall plunges into the watery depths.

G - The photographer's flash sets off the silvery color and tapered form of several bigeye trevallies (Caranx sexfasciatus) swimming in the depths.

DHIGGIRI KANDU

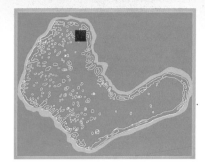

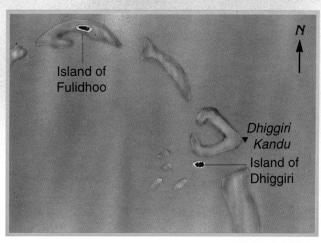

Island of
Fulidhoo

N

*Dhiggiri
Kandu*

Island of
Dhiggiri

0 m

30 m

40 m

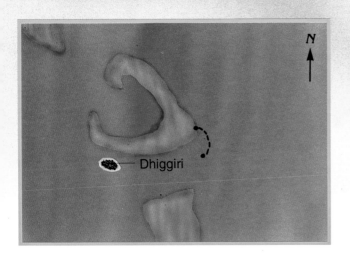

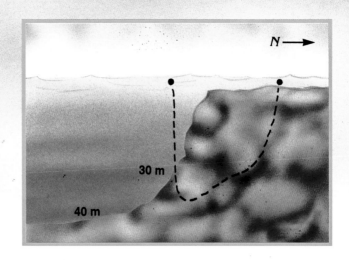

Dhiggiri

N

N

30 m

40 m

LOCATION

Dhiggiri Pass is located in the northeastern section of the Felidhu Atoll. Nearby islands include Dhiggiri, just inside the pass, and Alimathaa, a little farther to the south. Both islands have tourist villages.
The diving area is situated right in the outside left corner of the oceanic channel, facing east. To be more precise, it is the terrace that opens onto the sea just below the outside wall of the reef, which first descends 40-45 meters from the surface, then drops off to unfathomable depths. When the incoming current is strong, it is one of the best points for observing schools of pelagic fish.

DESCRIPTION OF THE DIVE

It is always a good idea to enter the water from the *dhoni* at least 50 meters north of the true corner of the channel and about 20 meters away from it, so that you can easily descend to the desired depth without being pushed too far into the atoll.
Once you have reached the terrace at a depth of 40 meters, if the current permits you can push to the drop-off and stay there in observation until your down-time and air reserves require you to come up. Keeping the wall to your right at all times, you will come to the entry of the pass,

A - This photograph is yet another testimony to the richness of the Maldivian seabed; hundreds of anthias swim around a colorful formation of alcyonarians.

B - These jacks, photographed from below, are moving out toward the pass drop-off.

C - A good diver following a turtle during a dive can offer excellent tips for beautiful photos.

D - The powerful currents that run through this part

of the atoll attract numerous pelagic fish such as barracudas, which during certain periods may form schools of hundreds of individuals.

E - Eagle rays are certainly among the most fascinating creatures in the underwater world; their wingspan can exceed 2 meters, while they may reach two and a half meters in length.

F - This close-up of a gray reef shark demonstrating all its power inspires a certain respect.

where you can let yourself be carried up to emerge under the support boat, which is waiting for the divers in the waters within the atoll.

Once you enter the pass you will see numerous horizontal cracks in the interior area, and on the bottom of the channel itself you will find true coral islands which rise up 7-10 meters from the sandy bottom.

Dhiggiri is famous among divers due to the great predators that ply its waters. Indeed, when the enormous mass of ocean water enters the atoll, the "lords of the sea" gather at the mouth of this sort of funnel, waiting for fish

F

E

G

which cannot fight against the violence of the salty flow and, at the mercy of the current, become easy prey.

At the edge of the drop-off you will see an imposing school of barracudas in compact formation, positioned side to side and apparently immobile, so that they seem attached to invisible threads, a marvelous silvery wall that reflects the rays of the sun. A little farther ahead is a group of jacks moving nervously at the edge of the drop-off.

They too are formidable predators, but here the sharks rule, and any wrong move could be fatal for them. In fact, as soon as one appears in the blue depths, gray sharks begin to arrive at the

edge of the drop-off, and from the open sea great hammerhead sharks often appear as well, with their long tails that seem to brush the water. Even mako sharks have been sighted in these waters, a certainly disquieting presence. Large schools of eagle rays circle at the water's surface.

You may easily encounter sea turtles swimming in the channel among the dense schools of reef fish. This dive is reserved for divers who have a great deal of experience in drift diving in deep water. Intermediate level divers can try this dive during slack water time between the periods when water is flowing into or out of the atoll: keep an eye on your pressure gauge!

PHOTOGRAPHY

Because there are large fish in this area, you will get best results using lenses from 20 to 28 millimeters. The flash should be used manually at half power, measuring background light and using suitable exposures.
The silvery scales of the jacks and barracudas reflect a great deal of light, so avoid taking photos in TTL mode.

G - Sometimes solitary hammerhead sharks (Sphyrna lewini) can be encountered in deeper water; the shape of their heads makes them easy to recognize.

KUDHI BOLI

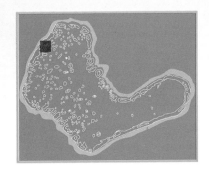

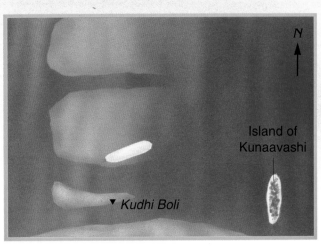

Island of
Kunaavashi

▼ Kudhi Boli

N

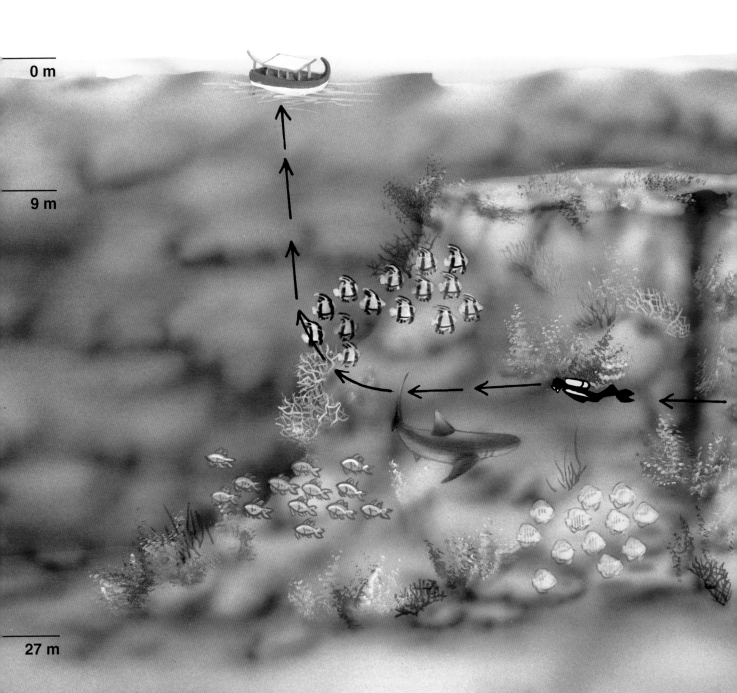

0 m

9 m

27 m

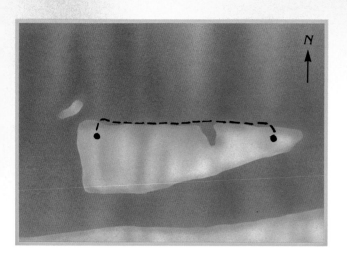

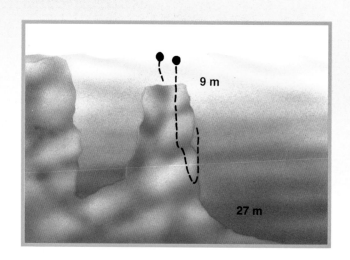

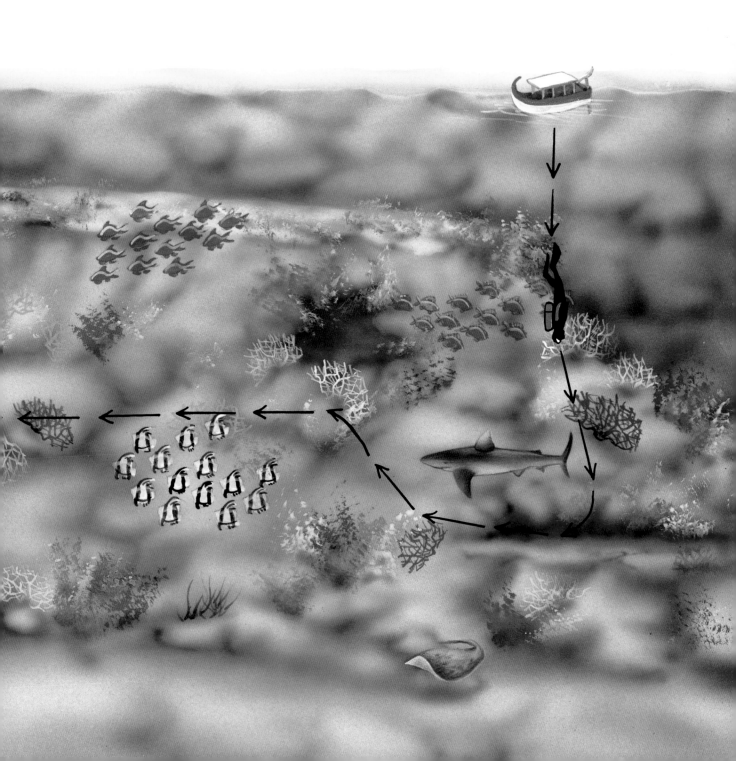

LOCATION

Kudhi Boli is located in the north-western area of the Felidhu Atoll. Nearby islands are Kunaavashi and another small island with no name, covered with low vegetation.
The *thila*, which is in the middle of an ocean channel, runs west to east for about 50 meters, and extends from a depth of 25 meters to 9 from the surface. A deep vertical cut runs through the center, with an opening passing through to the bottom.

DESCRIPTION OF THE DIVE

As the walls of the shoal are entirely covered by brilliantly colored alcyonarians, in order to best

appreciate its beauty you should dive when the current leaving the atoll swells the soft corals, significantly increasing their size and heightening their colors. You should enter the water at least 50 meters east of the shoal, so that the current will carry you exactly where you want to go. While the side walls are perpendicular to the sea floor, the western side, toward the open sea, ascends gradually, and it is thus possible to finish the dive by climbing back up the slope. This diving area is characterized by numerous red-orange, yellow and lilac alcyonarians. They are so thick that you cannot see the coral wall to which they are attached. In addition to soft corals, you will see large schools of

bannerfish, with their characteristic yellow and black stripes, located near the vertical crack which hides numerous soldierfish. The hole that goes through the wall is home to a group of saber squirrelfish and several coral groupers. You may see some whitetip sharks, a school of jacks and a few stingrays resting on the seabed. As this area is frequented by very few divers, the coral garden is perfectly intact, and you must be very careful, especially if you are a photographer, to avoid leaning against anything and to keep your position under control. Soft corals are very delicate, and all it takes is a little bump to break the base and thus cause them to die. This is a place where you really must walk on tiptoe.

A, C and D - The richness of Kudhi Boli lies in its alcyonarians. No other portion of the archipelago has such a high concentration of soft corals colonizing the walls of the reef. At certain times of the day when the corals are turgid with their polyps extended, the sight that greets divers is truly astounding.

B - At the base of the slope are large whip corals and dense schools of

masked bannerfish (Heniochus monoceros).

E - Areas not colonized by soft corals are taken over by hard corals; there are about 50 genera of hard corals on the Maldives. A one-eyed hawkfish (Paracirrhites arcatus) rests on a coral formation.

F - This red grouper seems camouflaged in the explosion of corals that covers the reef.

PHOTOGRAPHY

You'll certainly want to use an entire roll of film for Kudhiboli's explosion of colors. It is best to use lenses like the 15 mm *Nikonos* or even more extreme amphibious optical systems. Be very careful of the flash you use for seascape photos, as alcyonarians absorb a great deal of light. Bannerfish, which are not at all intimidated by the presence of divers, can be approached for full frame images which will be highly effective. The jacks are also excellent subjects, provided that you consider the reflecting power of their silvery scales.

G

E

H

F

G - Squirrelfish dart from the crevices. If divers come too close, they make threatening sounds similar to the crack of a whip. This one is submitting to the care of a cleaner fish (Labroides dimidiatus).

H - A stingray (Taeniura melanospilos) rises from the seabed, perhaps disturbed by the approach of a group of divers.

149

FULIDHOO OUTSIDE

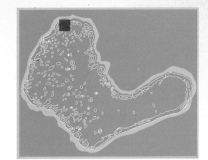

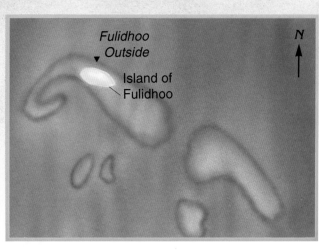

Fulidhoo
Outside

Island of
Fulidhoo

N

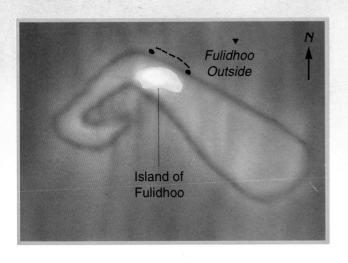

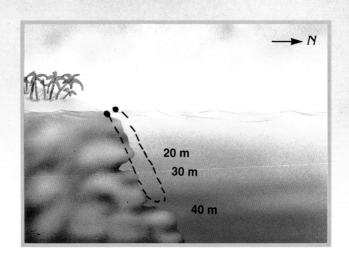

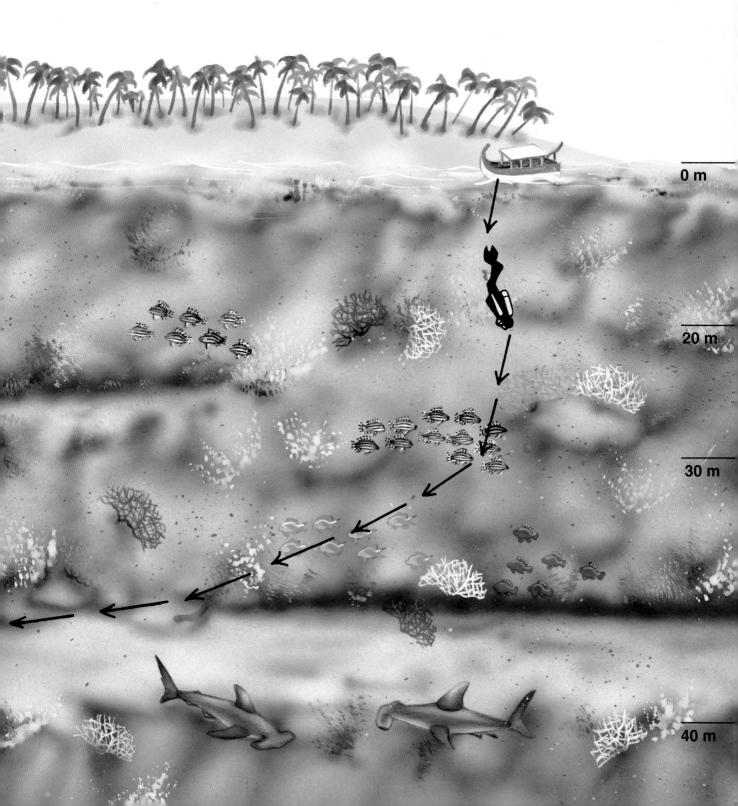

LOCATION

The diving area is situated at the far north end of the Felidhu Atoll, outside the coral reef. Nearby islands are Fulidhoo, inhabited by fishermen, and Dhiggiri, where there is a resort. This we will be exploring runs from the oceanic wall right below the island of Fulidhoo, descending from the surface vertically to an initial drop-off at a depth of about 40 meters, then, after a narrow terrace, plunging to unfathomable depths. At a depth of between 25 and 35 meters, the reef is broken by horizontal fissures which are not very deep but are rich with life.

DESCRIPTION OF THE DIVE

The most interesting part of the dive is certainly at the very center of the island of Fulidhoo. As there are always currents in this area, although very weak, you should enter the water to the left or the right of this point in order to reach the grotto area in a few minutes. After exploring the interior of the recesses, start emerging diagonally, keeping contact with the wall, until you end the dive on the island's emerging reef. This is the great oceanic channel that separates the Atoll of South Malé from that of Felidhu. Given its position characterized by movements of large masses of very deep water, you may meet up with anything in this area, especially large pelagic species. Stopping on the edge of the drop-off at a depth of 40 meters and facing the open sea, you can often see small groups of hammerheads. Sometimes an individual will leave the formation and approach divers. Large mako sharks, which should command a healthy respect, have been sighted along this wall. In the sandy areas of the plateau you may see leopard sharks resting on the bottom, always ready to flee rapidly if you come too close. Lobsters take shelter in the cavities, their long antennae continuously waving, along with a few morays with their constant

C - During this dive one may meet a rare inhabitant of the Maldivian seas: the leopard shark (Stegostoma fasciatum). It is easily recognizable by the spots on its body and its long tail.

D - This sea fan required dozens of years to reach this size.

E - The dark figure of a scuba diver contrasts with the light colors of some encrusting sponges and corals growing along the reef.

F - This whip coral was not able to grow in its normal vertical form and thus assumed a horizontal position.

G - A diver seems suspended over the yellow patch formed by a school of bluestriped snappers (Lutjanus kasmira).

H - Reviewing your videos is a way to broaden your knowledge of marine life.

companion the shrimp, intent on their cleaning work. On the wall, perpendicular to the current, grow colorful sea fans, around which parrotfish, groups of sweetlips and snappers go about their normal business. This dive does not require any special skill and can thus be enjoyed by all divers. Nevertheless, plan maximum depth based on your experience. As the water in this area is very clear, keep a constant eye on your computer in order to avoid being deceived by the good visibility and finding yourself too deep.

PHOTOGRAPHY

A 28 mm lens is recommended for this dive, in case you encounter a shark. If so, use the flash manually at half power so that the background will not be too dark. Using a 15 millimeter lens you can take beautiful photographs with sea fans in the foreground, appropriately illuminated with the sun in the background.

A, B - The outside wall of Fulidhoo, located in an oceanic channel between two atolls where the water is hundreds of meters deep, is one of the best places to encounter schools of hammerhead sharks (Sphyrna lewini), which often appear from the watery depths like phantoms.

SOUTH MALÉ ATOLL

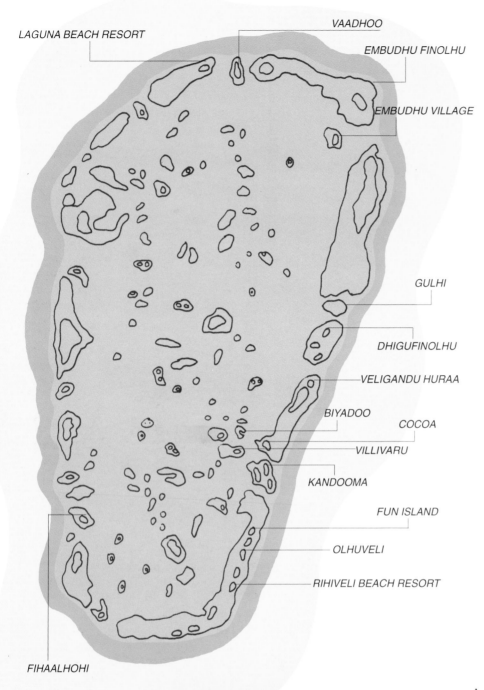

LAGUNA BEACH RESORT
VAADHOO
EMBUDHU FINOLHU
EMBUDHU VILLAGE
GULHI
DHIGUFINOLHU
VELIGANDU HURAA
BIYADOO
COCOA
VILLIVARU
KANDOOMA
FUN ISLAND
OLHUVELI
RIHIVELI BEACH RESORT
FIHAALHOHI

SOME RESORTS IN SOUTH MALÉ ATOLL

Heading south, the first island one sees when leaving Malé is **Vaadhoo**, open since 1978. It has 24 standard rooms and 7 luxurious cottages on the water, each one with a glass wall that looks out onto a picture postcard view. There is diving from a private pier, and about half its clientele is Asiatic.

Embudhu Finolhu, opened in 1983, has sand floors in all common areas. Tourists are housed in 26 chalets on the lagoon, with verandahs and direct access to the sea, and in 16 cottages on the beach. Hotel managed by the Tak group, with European and Japanese clientele.

Embudhu Village has 124 bungalows with red roofs emerging

B

from the thick vegetation, and is popular with a primarily German and French clientele.

Dhigufinolhu and **Veligandu Huraa** belong to the same company and are connected by a long wooden footbridge, in the center of which there is a bar.

Bushi, a third island connected to the other two in the same manner, houses the power house and desalinator, generators, staff quarters and the diving school.

Dhigu, the largest island, has 50 chalets and 14 high standard rooms.

E

F

A, B - The coralline sand that surrounds the islands has a characteristic whitish color, thus making the sea which laps against the beaches a beautiful turquoise blue.

C - The elegant structures of the island are perfectly integrated with the green vegetation. Well-kept flowerbeds can be seen around the common areas.

Palm Tree Island has 16 cottages. Both resorts offer a shuttle service that connects them to a snorkeling platform anchored in the middle of the lagoon.

Cocoa is a quite unique island where no concessions to luxury have been made except for the champagne. It has 8 rustic rooms with sand floors and coral walls, all finishing touches and furnishings in natural materials.

Biyadoo is preferred by the English for its comfort and Indian-style service. The hydroponic garden with its tropical vegetables and fruit is one of a kind.

Villivaru has beautiful private gardens surrounding each bungalow. Seen from the ocean, the vegetation is so thick that the island appears uninhabited.

Kandooma, on the eastern edge of the atoll, houses up to 122 visitors, primarily Germans, with modest standards.

Fun Island has 100 very spacious and well-finished rooms, with verandahs on the splendid beach. A long footbridge leads to the reef,

C

D

where one can enjoy snorkeling. Very good and discreet service, with entertainment and an excellent diving center.

Olhuveli, rebuilt in 1991 with 133 rooms, 13 of which are chalets on the lagoon.

Rihiveli Beach Resort has 47 simple but carefully furnished rooms with excellent service. At low tide a small desert island can be reached on foot.

Fihaalhohi, surrounded by white sandy beach, has 92 rooms. Mostly German clients.

Laguna Beach Resort was remodeled in 1991 and now has an international clientele, in 115 elegant rooms with tastefully furnished common areas and excellent service. Beautiful island.

D - The terrace bar of Fun Island, a tourist village located on the island of Bodufinolhu, overlooks the great lagoon crossed by a long bridge that leads to the end of the reef.

E - The pilework in the lower lagoon creates an ideal corner for relaxation during the hottest part of the day.

F - This aereal view shows the beautiful island of Velassaru and the confortable Laguna Beach Resort.

KUDA GIRI WRECK

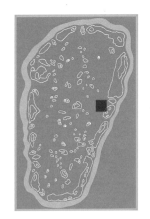

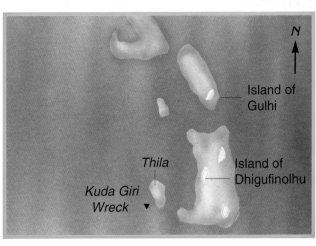

N

Island of
Gulhi

Thila

Island of
Dhigufinolhu

*Kuda Giri
Wreck* ▼

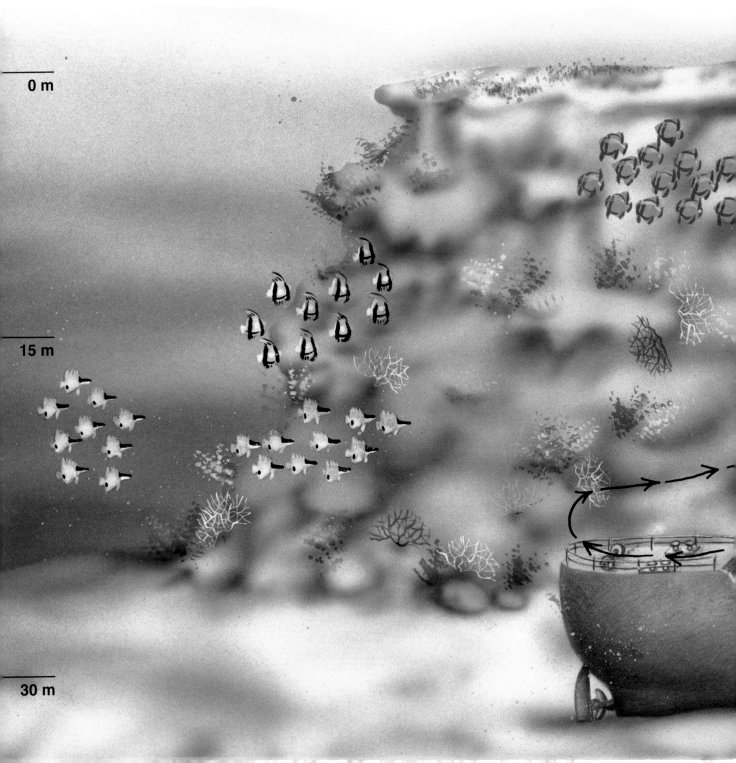

0 m

15 m

30 m

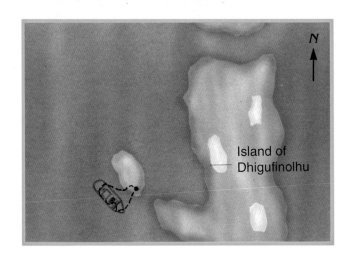

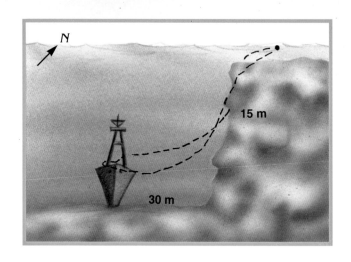

Island of
Dhigufinolhu

N

N

15 m

30 m

LOCATION

The *Kuda Giri wreck* is situated in the east central part of the South Malé Atoll. Nearby islands are Dhigufinolhu and Veliganduhuraa to the east, which are both tourist islands, and Gulhi to the north.
The ship is in navigating position, that is with the keel resting on the sand, at a depth of 30 meters. The upper structures are 15 meters from the surface. Sunk especially for divers, the boat is near a circular coral formation about 50 meters in diameter that extends up to the surface.

DESCRIPTION OF THE DIVE

The wreck is easy to locate, as it is very close to the *giri*, exactly to the southwest.
The dive can thus begin at any point on the reef, and once the wreck comes into sight you can leave the wall and explore it. The most interesting portions are near the propeller and quarterdeck. Once you have gone around the wreck, head toward the reef and spiral upwards, following the wall. The dive ends as you surface easily near the summit of the *giri*. Schools of batfish swim around the wreck and can be found along the walls of the giri itself. Inside the wreck you will find

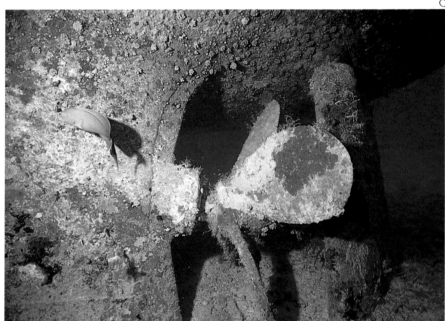

A - A comparison with a diver makes it possible to calculate the exact size of the hull with its keel resting on the sandy floor.

B - Exploring the inside of a wreck is always exciting, but one must be very cautious of the stability of the structures, which may have corroded and become dangerous.

C - Marine organisms, in particular corals and sponges, have taken over the structures of the wreck, creating palettes in a thousand colors. Here can be seen the propellor.

D - Despite the elegant appearance of this turkeyfish, which lightly moves its pectoral fins similar to feathers, it should be remembered that this fish is truly dangerous.

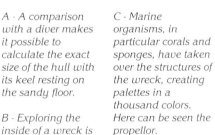

small groupers that come and go from among the cracks in the wreckage, while surgeonfish and butterflyfish move peacefully in what has become their home. You may easily encounter turkeyfish on the bridge showing off their splendid red and white colors. Curious coral aggregations have formed on the wreckage; if you look at them very carefully, you will discover an extremely varied and fascinating microcosm that includes small hawkfish (*Paracirrhites sp.*) perched on the branches of coral, and the tiny, brilliantly colored blennies peering out of their holes. There are also red and white striped shrimp (*Stenopus sp.*) and timid crabs:

you should begin appreciating these big little sights that Nature presents every day.

In the various recesses of the *giri* near the wreck are black corals, families of timid soldierfish *(Myripristis sp.)* and numerous anemones with their clownfish. The good position of the ship makes this dive appropriate for any level of expertise. Because of the weak currents and the relatively shallow depth, you can dive onto the wreck without any particular safety precautions.

PHOTOGRAPHY

In order to photograph as much of the wreck as possible, you need to use a wide-angle or even a fisheye lens. In both cases you should use natural lighting as much as possible. For macro photos, this is certainly a very "photogenic" area: you cannot possibly photograph all the little subjects that live here in just one dive.

E - Thousands of small glassfish live well protected inside the wreck. As can be seen in this photo the fish alive the encrusted metal structures of the ship with their brilliand silver and gold reflections.

F - Highlighted by a spotlight, which is always handy to have along during this type of dive, the encrustations reveal all their brilliant colors.

G - Like a company of soldiers, this compact school of batfish seems to be defending the wreck from invasions by strangers, especially divers.

H - Dives onto wrecks are usually reserved for expert divers, but anyone can dive on the Kuda Giri wreck due to its relative depth and the calm waters in which it lies.

I - This grouper seems to be fiercely defending the wreck chosen for its home.

160-161 This areal view shows the infinite colours typical of the Maldivian archipelago.

MALDIVIAN RESORTS

ALIMATHA AQUATIC RESORT
Safari Tours, S.E.K. No. 1,
Chandhani Magu, Malé
Tel Resort 450544
Tel Malé 323524
Fax Resort 450575
Fax Malé 322516

ANGAGA ISLAND RESORT
STO Koshi, 9 AmeeneeMagu,
Malé
Tel Resort 450520
Tel Malé 313636
Fax Resort 450520
Fax Malé 323115

**ARI BEACH RESORT
(DHIDHDHOO FINOLHU)**
52 Boduthakurufaanu Magu,
Malé
Tel Resort 450513
Tel Malé 321930
Fax Resort 450512
Fax Malé 327355

ASDHOO SUN ISLAND
H. Shoanary, Boduthakurufaanu
Magu, Malé
Tel Resort 445051
Tel Malé 322726
Fax Resort 445051
Fax Malé 324300

ATHURUGAU ISLAND RESORT
Voyages MaldivesPvt Ltd.
Fareedhee Magu, Malé
Tel Resort 450508
Tel Malé 324435
Fax Resort 450574
Fax Malé 324435

**AVI ISLAND RESORT
(VELIDHOO)**
G. Lifadhoo, Rukkediyaa Higun,
Malé
Tel Resort 450595
Tel Malé 322180
Fax Resort 450595
Fax Malé 325982

BANDOS ISLAND RESORT
H. Jazeera, Boduthakurufaanu
Magu, Malé
Tel Resort 440088
Tel Malé 322844
Fax Resort 443877
Fax Malé 321026

BAROS HOLIDAY RESORT
Universal Enterprises Ltd. 38
Orchid Magu, Malé
Tel Resort 442672
Tel Malé 322971
Fax Resort 443497
Fax Malé 322678

BATHALA ISLAND RESORT
H. Kinolhas, Abadhahfehi Magu,
Malé
Tel Resort 450587
Tel Malé 323323

Fax Resort 450558
Fax Malé 324628

BIYADOO ISLAND RESORT
Prabalaji Enterprises (Pvt) Ltd.,
H. Maarandhooge
Tel Resort 447171
Tel Malé 324699
Fax Resort 447272
Fax Malé 327014

BODUHITHI CORAL ISLE
Holiday Club Maldives, H.
Maizandhoshuge, Malé
Tel Resort 442637
Tel Malé 313938
Fax Resort 442634
Fax Malé 313939

BOLIFUSHI, ISLAND OF
Gateway Maldives Pte. Ltd,
Ameer Ahmed Magu,
Tel Resort 443517
Tel Malé 317526
Fax Resort 445924
Fax Malé 317529

**CLUB MED/FARUKOLHU
FUSHI**
1 Ibrahim HassanDidi Magu,
Majeedhee Bazaru
Tel Resort 444552
Tel Malé 322976
Fax Resort 441997
Fax Malé 322850

**COCOA ISLAND (MAKUNU
FUSHI)**
M. Gulisthaanuge, Malé
Tel Resort 443713
Tel Malé 322326
Fax Resort 441919
Fax Malé 322326

**CONCORDE REEF RESORT
(KUDA HURA)**
H. Jazeera, Boduthakurufanu
Mage, Malé
Tel Resort 445934
Tel Malé 327450
Fax Resort 444231
Fax Malé 321026

**DHIGUFINOLHU TOURIST
RESORT**
H. Athireege aage, Lotus Goalhi,
Malé
Tel Resort 443599
Tel Malé 327058
Fax Resort 443886
Fax Malé 327058

DIGGIRI TOURIST RESORT
Safari Tours, S.E.K. No. 1,
Chandhani Magu, Malé
Tel Resort 450592
Tel Malé 323524
Fax Resort 450592
Fax Malé 322516

**ELLAIDHOO TOURIST
RESORT**
Safari Tours, S.E.K. No. 1,
Chandhani Magu, Malé
Tel Resort 450514
Tel Malé 323524
Fax Resort 450586
Fax Malé 322516

**EMBUDHU FINOLHU ISLAND
RESORT**
Taj Maldives Pvt Ltd, 10
Medhuziyaaraiy Magu, Malé
Tel Resort 444451
Tel Malé 317530
Fax Resort 445925
Fax Malé 317530

EMBUDHU VILLAGE
H. Roanuge, Meheli Goalhi, Malé
Tel Resort 444776
Tel Malé 322212
Fax Resort 442673
Fax Malé 320614

ERIYADHU ISLAND RESORT
STO Trade Centre, 3rd Flr, Malé
Tel Resort 444487
Tel Malé 324933
Fax Resort 445926
Fax Malé 324943

FESDU FUN ISLAND
Universal Enterprises Ltd, 38
Orchid Magu, Malé
Tel Resort 450541
Tel Malé 322971
Fax Resort 450547
Fax Malé 322678

FIHALHOHI TOURIST RESORT
Journey World
Tel Resort 442903
Tel Malé 322016
Fax Resort 443803
Fax Malé 326606

**FULL MOON BEACH RESORT
(FURANA FUSHI)**
Universal Enterprises Ltd, 38
Orchid Magu, Malé
Tel Resort 441976
Tel Malé 323080
Fax Resort 441979
Fax Malé 322678

**FUN ISLAND RESORT
(BODU FINOLHU)**
Villa Building, Ibrahim Hassan
Didi Magu, Malé
Tel Resort 444558
Tel Malé 324478
Fax Resort 443958
Fax Malé 327845

GANGEHI ISLAND RESORT
Holiday Club, H.
Maizandhoshuge, Sosun Magu
Tel Resort 450505
Tel Malé 313938
Fax Resort 450506
Fax Malé 313939

**GASFINOLHU ISLAND
RESORT**
Imad's Agency, Chaandhanee
Magu, Malé
Tel Resort 442078
Tel Malé 323441
Fax Resort 445941
Fax Malé 322964

**GIRAAVARU TOURIST
RESORT**
Tel Resort 440440
Fax Resort 444818

HALAVELI HOLIDAY VILLAGE
Eastinvest (Pvt) Ltd, Malé
Tel Resort 450559
Tel Malé 322719
Fax Resort 450564
Fax Malé 323463

HELENGELI TOURIST VILLAGE
Nakhdha Store, Malé
Tel Resort 444615
Tel Malé 320988
Fax Resort 444615
Fax Malé 325150

**HEMBADHOO ISLAND
RESORT**
Transit Inn, Maveyo Magu, Malé
Tel Resort 443884
Tel Malé 322016
Fax Resort 441948
Fax Malé 326606

**HOLIDAY ISLAND
(DHIFFUSHI)**
Villa Building, Ibrahim Hassan
Didi Magu, Malé
Tel Resort 450011
Tel Malé 324478
Fax Resort 450022
Fax Malé 327845

HUDHUVELI BEACH RESORT
H. Jazeera, Boduthakurufaanu
Magu, Malé
Tel Resort 443391
Tel Malé 325529
Fax Resort 443982
Fax Malé 321026

IHURU TOURIST RESORT
Ihuru Investments Pvt Ltd,
Ameeru Ahmed Magu
Tel Resort 443502
Tel Malé 326720
Fax Resort 445933
Fax Malé 326700

**KANDOOMA TOURIST
RESORT**
Kandooma Malé Office, Orchid
Magu, Malé
Tel Resort 444452
Tel Malé 323360
Fax Resort 445948
Fax Malé 326880

KANIFINOLHU RESORT
Cyprea Ltd, 25
Boduthakurufaanu Magu, Malé
Tel Resort 443152
Tel Malé 322451
Fax Resort 444859
Fax Malé 323523

KUDAHITHI TOURIST RESORT
Holiday Club Maldives, H.
Maizandhoshuge, Malé
Tel Resort 444613
Tel Malé 313938
Fax Resort 441992
Fax Malé 313939

KUDARAH ISLAND RESORT
Holiday Club Maldives, H.
Maizandhoshuge, Malé
Tel Resort 450549
Tel Malé 313938
Fax Resort 450550
Fax Malé 313939

**KURAMATHI TOURIST
RESORT**
Universal Enterprises Ltd, 38
Orchid Magu, Malé
Tel Resort 450540
Tel Malé 322971
Fax Resort 450556
Fax Malé 322678

**KUREDHDHOO ISLAND
RESORT**
Champa Trade & Travel,
Ahmadhee Bazaar, Malé
Tel Resort 230337
Tel Malé 321751
Fax Resort 230332
Fax Malé 326544

**KURUMBA VILLAGE
(VIHAMANA FUSHI)**
Universal Enterprises Ltd, 38
Orchid Magu, Malé
Tel Resort 442324
Tel Malé 322971
Fax Resort 443885
Fax Malé 322678

**LAGUNA BEACH RESORT
(VELASSARU)**
Universal Enterprises Ltd, 38
Orchid Magu, Malé
Tel Resort 443042
Tel Malé 322971
Fax Resort 443041
Fax Malé 322678

**LHOHIFUSHI TOURIST
RESORT**
Altaf Enterprises, Ibrahim Hassan
Didi Magu, Malé
Tel Resort 441909
Tel Malé 323378
Fax Resort 441908
Fax Malé 324783

LILY BEACH RESORT
Lily Hotel, Chandhanee Magu,
Malé
Tel Resort 450013
Tel Malé 317464
Fax Resort 450646
Fax Malé 327466

**MAAYAFUSHI TOURIST
RESORT**
H. Luxwood 1, Upstairs,
Boduthakurufaanu Magu
Tel Resort 450588
Tel Malé 320097
Fax Resort 450568
Fax Malé 326658

**MACHCHAFUSHI ISLAND
RESORT**
Ocean View Shop No: 1, Malé
Tel Resort 450615
Tel Malé 327849
Fax Resort 450618
Fax Malé 327277

MADOOGALI RESORT
Medhuziyaaraiy Magu Magu,
Malé
Tel Resort 450581
Tel Malé 317984
Fax Resort 450554
Fax Malé 317974

MAKUNUDU ISLAND
Sunland Travel Pvt. Ltd
Tel Resort 446464
Tel Malé 324658
Fax Resort 446565
Fax Malé 325543

MEERU ISLAND RESORT
Champa Trade & Travels,
Ahmadhee Bazaar, Malé
Tel Resort 443157
Tel Malé 326545
Fax Resort 445946
Fax Malé 326544

**MIRIHI MARINA LUXURY
RESORT**
3 Silver Star, Haveeree Higun,
Malé
Tel Resort 450500
Tel Malé 325448
Fax Resort 450501
Fax Malé 325448

MOOFUSHI ISLAND RESORT
Tel Resort 450517
Tel Malé 326141
Fax Resort 450509
Fax Malé 326141

**NAKATCHAFUSHI TOURIST
RESORT**
Universal Entrerprises Ltd, 38
Orchid Magu, Malé
Tel Resort 443847
Tel Malé 322971
Fax Resort 442665
Fax Malé 322678

**NIKA HOTEL
(KUDA FOLHUDHOO)**
P.O. Box 2076, 10 Fareedhee
Magu, Malé
Tel Resort 450516
Tel Malé 325087
Fax Resort 450577
Fax Malé 325097

**OCEAN REEF CLUB
(GAN, SEENU ATOLL)**
Phoenix Hotel & Resorts Pvt Ltd,
Tel Malé 323181
Fax Malé 325499

OLHUVELI VIEW HOTEL
P.O. Bag 72
Tel Resort 441957
Tel Malé
Fax Resort 445942
Fax Malé

**PALM TREE ISLAND
(VELIGANDU HURAA)**
H. Athireege aage, Lotus Goalhi,
Malé
Tel Resort 443882
Tel Malé 327058
Fax Resort 440009
Fax Malé 327058

**PARADISE ISLAND
(LANKAN FINOLHU)**
Villa Building, Ibrahim Hassan
Didi Magu, Malé
Tel Resort 440011
Tel Malé 324478
Fax Resort 440022
Fax Malé 327845

RANGALI ISLAND RESORT
Crown Company Pte Ltd, P.O.
Box 2034, Malé
Tel Resort 450629
Tel Malé 322432
Fax Resort 450619
Fax Malé 324009

RANNALHI TOURIST VILLAGE
H. Kinolhas, Abadhahfehi Magu,
Malé
Tel Resort 442688
Tel Malé 323323
Fax Resort 442035
Fax Malé 324628

**RANVEVLI BEACH RESORT
(VILINGILIVARU)**
Holiday Club Maldives, H.
Maizandhoshuge, Malé
Tel Resort 450570
Tel Malé 313938
Fax Resort 450523
Fax Malé 313939

**REETHI RAH RESORT
(MEDHU FINOLHU)**
M. Shaazeewin,Fareedhee Magu,
Malé
Tel Resort 441905
Tel Malé 323758
Fax Resort 441906
Fax Malé 328842

**RIHIVELI BEACH RESORT
(MAHAANA ELHI HURAA)**
Jamaal Store, Ahmadhee Bazar
Tel Resort 443731
Tel Malé 322421
Fax Resort 440052
Fax Malé 322964

**SONEVAFUSHI
(KUNFUNADHOO)**
Bunny Holdings, H. Shoanary,
Malé
Tel Resort 230304
Tel Malé 326686
Fax Resort 230374
Fax Malé 324660

TARI VILLAGE (KANU HURAA)
Phoenix Hotels & Resorts Pvt Ltd,
Malé
Tel - Fax Resort 440012
Tel Malé 323181
Fax Malé 325499

**THULHAAGIRI ISLAND
RESORT**
H. Jazeera, Boduthakurufaanu
Magu, Malé
Tel Resort 445929
Tel Malé 322844
Fax Resort 445939
Fax Malé 321026

**THUNDUFUSHI ISLAND
RESORT**
Voyages Maldives Pvt Ltd,
Fareedhee Magu, Malé
Tel Resort 450597
Tel Malé 324435
Fax Resort 450515
Fax Malé 324435

**TWIN ISLAND
(MAAFUSHIVARU)**
Universal Enterprises Ltd, 38
Orchid Magu, Malé
Tel Resort 450596
Tel Malé 322971
Fax Resort 450524
Fax Malé 322678

VAADHOO DIVING PARADISE
H. Maarandhooge (Irumathee
Bai), Malé
Tel Resort 443976
Tel Malé 325844
Fax Resort 443397
Fax Malé 325846

VABBINFARU (BANYAN TREE)
Dhirham Travel & Chandelling,
Faamudheyri Magu, Malé
Tel Resort 443147
Tel Malé 323369
Fax Resort 443843
Fax Malé 324752

VAKARUFALHI ISLAND RESORT
Champa Trade & Travel, Ahmadhee Bazaar, Malé
Tel Resort 450004
Tel Malé 321751
Fax Resort 450007
Fax Malé 314150

VELIGANDU ISLAND
Crown Company Pte Ltd, P.O.

Box 2034, Malé
Tel Resort 450594
Tel Malé 322432
Fax Resort 450519
Fax Malé 324009

VILAMENDHU RESORT
Vision Maldives, STO Trade Centre, 3rd Flr, Malé
Tel Resort 450637
Tel Malé 322417

Fax Resort 450639
Fax Malé 324943

VILLIVARU ISLAND RESORT
Prabalaji Enterprises Pvt Ltd, H. Maarandhooge, Malé
Tel Resort 447070
Tel Malé 324699
Fax Resort 447272
Fax Malé 327014

ZIYAARAIYFUSHI TOURIST RESORT
c/o Kaimoo Travels
Tel Resort 443088
Tel Malé 322212
Fax Resort 441910

POSITION OF THE MAJOR PROTECTED DIVE SITES IN THE MALDIVES

Maldives has designated 15 popular dive sites as protected areas. Within these protected areas the following activities are prohibited:
1. Anchoring (except in an emergency).
2. Coral or sand mining.
3. Rubbish dumping.
4. Removal of any natural object or living creature.
5. Fishing of any kind (e.g. for sharks, reef fish, or aquariumu fish) with the exception of traditional livebait fishing.
6. Any other activity which may cause damage to the area or its associated marine life.

MALE' ATOLL

1. Makunudhoo Channel.
West of Makunudhoo. Northwestern side of North Malé Atoll. 04° 33'N, 73° 22'E Alternative names: - Kudafaru, Saddle, Himmiya Falhu.

2. Rasfari Outside. West side of North Malé Atoll. Outer reef of Rasfari Island 04° 24'N, 73° 20'E. Alternative name: - Rasfari Corner.

3. H.P. Reef.
West of Thanburudhoo. Western side of North Malé Atoll. Channel between Girifushi and Himmafushi. 04° 19'N, 73° 34.5' E. Alternative names: Girifushi Thila, Thanburudhoo Thila.

4. Banana Reef.
West of Full Moon Resort. Southeastern par of North Malé Atoll. 04° 14.5'N, 73° 32'E. Alternative names: Gaathugiri, Aiydhashugiri, Bodu Banana.

5. Giravaru Kuda Haa.
Inside south end of North Malé Atoll. Approximaely 500 meters northwest of Giravaru. 04° 13'N, 73° 24.5E'. Alternative names: Rainbow, Kuda Haa.

6. Lion's Head. South end of North Malé Atoll. Middle of Thila Falhu Reef, facing Vaadoo channel. 04° 11'N, 73° 25.5'E. Alternative name: Miyaruvani

7. Hans Hass Place.
Southern end of North Malé Atoll. Middle of Gulhi Falhu reef, facing Vaadoo channel. 04° 10.5'N, 73° 28'E. Alternative names: Kikki Reef, Dragon's Mouth.

8. Emboodhoo Channel.
Northeast side of South Malé Atoll. Due east of Emboodhoo. 04° 05'N, 73° 32'E. Alternative name: Emboodhoo Kandu.

9. Guaridhoo Channel.
Eastern side of South Malé Atoll. Two Channel south of Guraidhoo. 03° 54'N, 73° 28'E. Alternative name: Guraidhoo Corner, Guraidhoo Kanduolhi.

ARI ATOLL.

1. Maaya Thila. Inside Ari Atoll. Northwest of Maayaafushi. 04° 05'N, 72° 51.5'E. Alternative name: Maayaafushi Thila.

2. Orimas Thila. East side of Ari Atoll. Southwest of Maagau Island. 03° 59'N, 72° 57'E. Alternative name: Maagau Thila.

3. Fish Head. Inside Ari Atoll. South southwest from Mushimasmingili Island. 03° 57.5'N, 72° 55'E. Alternative names: Mushimasmingili Thila, Shark Thila.

4. Kuda Rah Thila.
Southeastern part of Ari Atoll. Between Kuda Rah and Dhigu Rah. 03° 34'N, 72° 55'E. Alternative name: Pink Shark Thila.

VAAVU ATOLL.

1. Dhevana Kandu. Westside of Vaavu Atoll. third channel south of Alimatha. 03° 35'N, 73° 30'E. Alternative name: Miyaru Kandu.

LHAVIYANI ATOLL.

1. Fushifaru Thila.
Northeastern side of Lhaviyani Atoll. Channel southeast of Fushifaru. 05° 29'N, 73° 31'E. Alternative name: Fushivaru Thila.

PROVISIONAL LIST OF KNOWN SHIP-WRECKS IN THE MALDIVES

Government permission must be obtained before making wreck dives outside tourism zone.

1. DHAPPARU: Haa-Alif Atoll. On the north-eastern reef of this island there are stones other than coral, which is said to have been on board a wooden ship that ran aground here. The identity of the ship or the date of the wreck is not known. These stones, according to stories were used as ballast on that ship.

2. FILLADHOO: Haa-Alif Atoll. "Captain Pentalis" (3,132 tons) was wrecked on the reef of this island on 4 June 1963. She was not re-floated.

3. HATHIFUSHI: Haa-Alif Atoll. A ship of unknown identity ran aground near this island on 30 July 1917.

4. KADUFUSHI: Haa-Alif Atoll. A steel ship named "Oceano" was wrecked on the reef of this island on 19 July 1917. She was 4,657 tons and sailing from Calcutta to River Plate with a cargo of jute, tea and gunnies. She was of British registry.

5. RUFFUSHI: Haa-Dhaal Atoll. A wooden ship "Royal Family" of Liverpool registry was wrecked on the reef of this island on 19 August 1868. She was 1,750 tons, with a crew of 34 travelling from Aden to Callao on ballast. She was a total loss.

6. MAKUNUDHOO: Haa-Dhaal Atoll. The following ships were wrecked on the reef of this island: (1) "Persia Merchant" in August 1658; (2) English ship "Hayston" in 1819; (3) "George Reid" on 26 September 1872.

7. FARUKOLHU-FUNADHOO: Shaviayani Atoll. A yacht named "Happy" ran aground on the reef of an islet in the lagoon of this island on 27 January 1981 and she was re-floated on 5 February 1981.

8. GOIDHOO: Shaviyani Atoll. A wooden vessel of unknown identity ran aground on the eastern reef of this island on 24 December 1979. She was not re-floated.

9. FULHADHOO: Baa Atoll. "Corbin" was wrecked on the reef of this island on 2 July 1602 with Pyrard de Laval on board, who wrote a full description of the Maldives at that time in his book "Voyages of Pyrard de Laval".

10. DIFFUSHI: Lhaviyani Atoll. A ship destined to Malé from Colombo ran aground on this reef on 22 January 1966. She was named "City of Victoria". This ship was re-floated on 7 March 1966 and re-named "Dhiffushimaadhoo".

11. MALE': Kaaf Atoll. m.v. "Dynasty Utheemu" ran aground on the eastern reef on 15 June 1984. She was re-floated on 14 August 1984. m.v. "Pacific Rover" ran aground on the same point on 21 March 1985 and was re-floated on 5 May 1985.

12. DHIFFUSHI: Kaaf Atoll. On the reef of this island the folowing baggalas were wrecked: (1) "Dheen Ganja" in 1898; (2) "Deyla" in 1903; (3) "Jandar" in 1911.

13. EBOODHOO-FINOLHU: Kaaf Atoll. "Golden Dragon 202" ran onto the reef of this island on 31 December 1981. She was re-floated the next day.

14. FURANAFUSHI: Kaaf Atoll. On 25 December 1923, in a severe storm a baggala which had come from Colombo and was with full cargo struck the reef of this island and sank. No lives were lost.

15. GAAFARU: Kaaf Atoll. There are many ship wrecks on this reef and vicinity. The identified ones are: (1) 1,174 ton iron ship "Aracan" with 41 crew sailing from Rangoon to London with general cargo and 9 passengeres ran aground on 12 August 1873. She was registered at Glasgow and was a total loss; (2) 363 ton barque "Clan Alpine" which was wrecked on this reef in October 1879 on her way to Bombay from Mauritius with a cargo of sugar. She was a wooden barque and was registred at Leith. She was a total loss; (3) 1,012 ton s.s. "Sea Gull" which was wrecked on this reef in 1879 had a crew of 32 and was sailing from Calcutta to London with general cargo and 3 passengers. She was a sailing iron ship registred at Leith and was total loss; (4) "Erlangen" which ran aground on this reef on 21 August 1895; (5) s.s. "Crusader" which was wrecked here in 1905 was sailing with a cargo of sugar; (6) 863 ton "Lady Christine" of Panamanian registration which was wrecked here on 16 April 1974.

16. HELEGELI: Kaaf Atoll. 1,397 ton "Swiss" ran aground on this reef on 29 May 1890 and was a total loss. She was sailing from Pondicherry to Marsailles and was of steel. A sailing vessel owned by the Maldivian Government called "Dharuma" ran aground on the reef of this island on 24 January 1962. She too was a total loss.

17. HULHULE: Kaaf Atoll. m.v. "Maldive Victory" sank near the reef of this island on 13 February 1981. She carried a crew of 35 and the cargo consisted of 65 drums of oil and 1080 tons of general cargo. The crew was saved. The ship was built in 1958 and had a gross tonnage of 1,407. The depth at which she rests is 118 feet (36 metres).

18. BODU BADOS: Kaaf Atoll. A wooden vessel which was used as a sailing ODI and later mechanised and named "Dhandehelu" ran aground on the reef of this island on 13 May 1982. It was a total loss.

19. KURAMATHI: Alif Atoll. 965 ton ship "Reinder" with a crew of 26, sailing from Mauritius to Galle on ballast was wrecked on the south-west point of this reef on 29 May 1868. She was a total loss. Her port of registration was Liverpool.

20. HIGAAKULHI: Vaavu Atoll. A ship named "Pioneer" which was on her way from Colombo to Malé with general cargo ran aground on the reef of this island on 13 May 1958. She was not re-floated.

21. MADUVVARI: Meemu Atoll. A ship named "Ravestin" with a cargo of gold ran aground on the reef of this island on 9 May 1726.

22. MAALHAVELI: Meemu Atoll. "Prazere Algeria" was wrecked on the reef of this island on 16 March 1844 with the loss of 11 lives. She was sailing from Lisbon to Goa with 104 passengers and convicts. 11 lives were lost. Her port of registration was Lisbon.

23. KOLHUVAARIYAAFUSHI: Meemu Atoll. A mosque was built on this island by Sultan Ghazi Muhammed Thakurufaanu (1573-1585) with the remains of his vessel "Kalhuohfummi", which was wrecked on the reef of this island on her last voyage to southern atolls.

24. HIMITHI: Faaf Atoll. French ship "Duras" was wrecked on the reef of this island on 12 April 1777.

25. KUDAHUVADHOO: Dhaal Atoll. 1,339 ton iron ship "Liffey" ran aground on the reef of this island on 3 August 1879. She was sailing from Mauritius to Calcutta on ballast and she had 3 passengers. Her port of registry was London. She was a total loss. "Utheemu I" was wrecked on the reef of this island on 15 July 1960. She was a total loss.

26. VELIGADU: Thaa Atoll. A ship named "Adonis" was wrecked here in July 1835. It was a total loss.

27. MAAVAH: Laamu Atoll. A barque "Franceois", with a crew of 22 was wrecked on the reef of this island on 3 June 1873. She was sailing from Bourbon to Calcutta and was registered at Bordeaux.

28. ISDHOO: Laamu Atoll. 5,583 ton "Lagan Bank" of British registration, with a cargo of jute and guinnies, was wrecked on the reef of this island on 13 January 1938. A Nationalist Chinese fishing vessel named "Yuang Haing" ran aground on the reef on 11 February 1969. She re-floated and re-named "Isdhoo Muli".

29. RAAVERREHAA: Gaaf-Alif Atoll. A ship of unknown identity ran aground on the reef of this island in 1883.

30. VILIGILI: Gaaf-Alif Atoll. A liner with about 700 passengers ran around on the nearby reef on 24 May 1902. This ship was not re-floated. Another ship by the name "Dhaalathaa" was wrecked on the neary reef, Ekafaru, on 15 Agust 1947. She was re-floated on 26 October 1948. A Panama registered vessel named "Kurtia I" ran aground on the same reef on 11 March 1978 and was re-floated on 23 April 1978.

31 KOLAMAAFUSHI: Gaaf-Alif Atoll. A wooden ship called "Surat" was wrecked on the south-east of this island in 1802.

32. MAAMUTAA: Gaaf-Alif Atoll. A ship by the name "Umaana", which was on her way from Calcutta to Africa, was wrecked on the reef of this island on 15 May 1903. A Greek ship "Nicolaos Embricas" of 8,450 tons with a cargo of jute, tea, gunnies and cotton ran aground on this reef on 15 May 1969. The ship was cut and the rear part of it was re-floated.

33. LONUDHOO: Gaaf-Dhaal Atoll. A ship of unknown identity ran aground on the reef of this island in 1896. The cargo on board was mainly textiles.

34. MAGUDHDHUVAA: Gaaf-Dhaal Atoll. Nationalist Chinese fishing vessel named "Ju Yung No. 1" ran aground

on the reef of this island on 15 February 1971. She was re-floated and re-named "Magudhdhoo".

35. HITHADHOO: Seenu Atoll. 5,583 ton steel ship "British Loyalty" was wrecked on the south-western reef of this island on 9 March 1944.

SHIP-WRECKS WHOSE EXACT LOCATION IS UNKNOWN

1. "Tranquabar", bound to Colombo with a cargo of cloth was wrecked near Malé on 29 January 1797. She was a total loss.
2. A French vessel of unknown identy was wrecked in an unknown area within the Maldives in 1806.
3. "Europa" with a cargo of arms and cloth and a crew of 29 was wrecked in the Southern Atolls on 23 May 1812.
4. "Hayston" with a cargo of metals, wine, glass and spice was wrecked in Malé Atoll in 1819.
5. "Vicissitude" sailing from Mauritius to Ceylon was wrecked in Ihavandu-fulu atoll (Ihavandhippolhu now included within Haa-Alif Atoll)

in 1836. She was a total loss.
6. "James McInroy" was wrecked in the Maldives in 1837. The location is unknown.
7. "St. Clair Paramatta" was wrecked in Haddummathi atoll (Laamu Atoll) in 1855. She had a crew of 11.
8. "Spirit", with a crew of 9 was wrecked in Gaaf-Alif and Gaaf-Dhaal Atolls in September 1856.
9. "George Reid" of 115 tons with a crew of 19 sailing from London to Galle on ballast was wrecked on the south-western barrier reef of Miladhummadulu atoll (Shaviyani and Noonu Atolls) on 25 September 1872. She was registered at Bridgewater and was an iron sailing ship. She was a total loss.
10. "Aegean" of 836 tons (a sailing iron ship) with a crew of 26 sailing from Sourabaya to Amsterdam with cotton, tobacco and sugar was wrecked at Gaaf-Alif and Gaaf-Dhaal Atolls on 4 May 1873. She was registered at Leith and was a partial loss.
11. "L'Ecureuil" of 204 tons sailing from Buenos Aires to

Singapore on ballast with a crew of 10 was wrecked "on the coral reefs of One-and-a-HalfDegree Channel". She was a wooden brig and was a total loss. Her port of registry was Bayonne.
12. "Adeline" of 145 tons sailing from Mauritius to Colombo with a cargo of sugar and empty casks was wrecked in Gaaf-Alif and Gaaf-Dhaal Atolls on 8 November 1874. There were 2 passegers on board. She was a three masted iron schooner registered at Port Louis and was a total loss.
13. "Consett" of 1,105 tons sailing from Bassein to Port Said with a crew of 28 was wrecked on the north-east edge of Gaaf-Alif and Gaaf-Dhall Atolls on 7 May 1880. She was an iron sailing ship registered at Newcastle and was a total loss.
14. "Khedive Ismail" of 7,513 tons sailing from Mombasa to Colombo with troops was sunk in enemy action in the Indian Ocean near Maldives (00 degrees 57 minutes 00 seconds North, 72 degrees 16 minutes 00 seconds East). 1,297 lives were lost.

MARINE PRODUCTS PROHIBITED FOR EXPORT FROM THE MALDIVES

- Black Coral
- Trochus shell
- Lobster
- Lobster meat
- Black coral necklace
- Boulder coral
- Branching coral
- Coral

- Bait fish used for pole and line fishing
- Big eye scad (less than 6")
- Mother of pearl shells
- Dolphin
- Whales
- Couch (triton) shell
- Rays (from 25 June 1995)

- Eels (from 25 June 1995)
- Pufferfish (from 25 June 1995)
- Parrotfish (from 25 June 1995)
- Ray skin (from 01 January 1996)
- Turtle, turtle shells and

turtle shell products (from 01 January 1996)

MARINE FAUNA PROHIBITED TO CATCH, KILL OR TO BE TAKEN WITHIN THE EXCLUSIVE ECONOMIC ZONE OF MALDIVES

- Dolphin
- Whales
- Berried female lobster and

those with less than 25 centimetres in total lenght
- Conch (triton) shell

- Giant clams
- Black coral
- Whale shark

- Humphead wrasse
- Marine turtles (for ten years from 25 June 1995)

SOME CRUISING VESSELS OF THE MALDIVES

Allaudeen
Beds: 4
Cabin: 1
Operator: Quest Enterprises
Ltd., H. Hickory, Malé
Tel. 323014
Fax 323774

Baraabaru
Beds: 11
Cabin: 5
Operator: Sea Explorers
Diving School
Tel. 316172
Fax 316783

Blue Marlin
Beds: 14
Cabin: 7
Operator: Voyages Maldives
Pvt. Ltd.
Tel. 322019
Fax 325336

Bodumahora
Beds: 14
Cabin: 6
Operator: Detours
Tel. 323181
Fax 325499

Dhandehelu-2
Beds: 12
Cabin: 6
Operator: Detours
Tel. 323181
Fax 325499

Discovery
Beds: 12
Cabin: 3
Operator: Cyprea Pvt. Ltd.
Tel. 326688
Fax 323523

Dolphin
Beds: 8
Cabin: 4
Operator: Seafari Adventures
Monza - Italy
Tel. 39-39-329338
Fax 39-39-328946
E-mail seafari_maldives@iol.it

Flying fish
Beds: 14
Cabin: 7
Operator: Panorama Maldives
Pvt. Ltd.
Tel. 327066
Fax 326542

Get Wet 1
Beds: 8
Cabin: 4
Tel. 323014
Fax 323774
Tel. Germany 49-6227-1030
Fax Germany 49-6227-1037

Green Peace
Beds: 8
Cabin: 1
Operator: Voyages Maldives

Pvt. Ltd.
Tel. 322019
Fax 325336

Gulfaam
Beds: 16
Cabin: 8
Operator: Voyages Maldives
Pvt. Ltd.
Tel. 322019
Fax 325336

Hagern
Beds: 17
Cabin: 7
Operator: Ahmed Moosa, Ma.
Champaamaage
Fax 445946

Hammerhead
Beds: 12
Cabin: 6
Operator: Manfred
Fax 49-880-91889

Hammerhead-2
Beds: 17
Cabin: 7
Operator: Siegfried Berth
Tel. 49-61-5184437
Fax 49-61-5184426

Huvani
Beds: 12
Cabin: 6
Operator: Seafari Adventures
Monza - Italy
Tel. 39-39-329338
Fax 39-39-328946
E-mail seafari_maldives@iol.it

Jaariya
Beds: 22
Cabin: 11
Operator: Interlink Maldives
Tel. 313537
Fax 313538

Kaamiyaab
Beds: 8
Cabin: 2
Operator: Quest Enterprises
Ltd., H. Hickory, Malé
Tel. 323014
Fax 323774

Keema
Beds: 12
Cabin: 6
Operator: Interlink Maldives
Tel. 313537
Fax 313538

Kethi
Beds: 14
Cabin: 7
Operator: Voyages Maldives
Pvt. Ltd.
Tel. 322019
Fax 325336

Koimala
Beds: 14
Cabin: 7

Operator: Seafari Adventures
Monza - Italy
Tel. 39-39-329338
Fax 39-39-328946
E-mail seafari_maldives@iol.it

Kudhiboli
Beds: 10
Cabin: 5
Operator: Detours
Tel. 323181
Fax 325499

Kureli
Beds: 14
Cabin: 6
Operator: Detours
Tel. 323181
Fax 325499

Madivaru III
Beds: 13
Cabin: 8
Operator: Seafari Adventures
Monza - Italy
Tel. 39-39-329338
Fax 39-39-328946
E-mail seafari_maldives@iol.it

Madivaru 7
Beds: 12
Cabin: 6
Operator: Seafari Adventures
Monza - Italy
Tel. 39-39-329338
Fax 39-39-328946
E-mail seafari_maldives@iol.it

Mandhu
Beds: 14
Cabin: 6
Operator: Detours
Tel. 323181
Fax 325499

Muna
Beds: 20
Cabin: 6
Operator: Ahmed Moosa, Ma.
Champaamaage
Fax 445946

Nasruali
Beds: 16
Cabin: 8
Operator: Fun Tours Trade &
Travel Pvt. Ltd.
Tel. 327755
Fax 324559

Nasruman
Beds: 8
Cabin: 4
Operator: Fun Tours Trade &
Travel Pvt. Ltd.
Tel. 327755
Fax 324559

Nasruveli
Beds: 14
Cabin: 7
Operator: Fun Tours
Tel. 327755
Fax 324559

Panorama
Beds: 10
Cabin: 5
Operator: Panorama Maldives
Pvt. Ltd., Malé
Tel. 327066
Fax 326542

Pioneer
Beds: 6
Cabin: 3
Operator: Voyages Maldives
Pvt. Ltd.
Tel. 322019
Fax 325336

Saarah
Beds: 16
Cabin: 7
Operator: Hussain Afeef
Fax 445946

Sea Canary
Beds: 5
Cabin: 1
Operator: Voyages Maldives
Pvt. Ltd.

Sea Coral
Beds: 12
Operator: Voyages Maldives
Tel. 322019
Fax 325336

Sea Farer
Beds: 9
Cabin: 4
Operator: Voyages Maldives
Tel. 322019
Fax 325336

Sea Pleasure
Beds: 8
Cabin: 2
Operator: Sea Explorers
Diving School
Tel. 316172
Fax 316783

Sea Ranger
Beds: 8
Cabin: 1
Operator: Voyages Maldives
Pvt. Ltd.

Suvaasaa 2
Beds: 12
Cabin: 4
Operator: Detours
Tel. 323181
Fax 325499

Voyager I
Beds: 7
Cabin: 1
Operator: Voyages Maldives
Pvt. Ltd.
Tel. 322019
Fax 325336

168 An elegant sea turtle, illuminated by the sun rays filtering through the sea surface crosses the deep blue waters of the Maldives.

Cover
A diver carefully approaches an enormous branch of red coral outstretched in the waters off Goidhoo.
Photograph by Claudio Cangini

Back cove - top
Lively anthias dart about on the coral reef; the bed is covered with multicoloured alcyonarians, contrasting with the deep blue of the sea of Kudhi Boli.
Photograph by Claudio Cangini

Back cover - bottom
The cruise ship Koi Mala sails the blue waters of the Maldives taking divers to unique diving spots with extraordinarily rich sea beds.
Photograph by Seafari

All photographs are by Claudio Cangini except for the following: Marcello Bertinetti/ Archivio White Star: pages 79 B,E; 87 E; 154. Kurt Amsler: pages 9;19 A; 24 A; 25 E; 50 A; 79 F; 160-161. Baro Resort: page 26 C. Gianluca Beretta / Kudaram Resort: pages 12 A;86 B; 86-87. Claudio Bertasini: pages 79 D; 84 A; 118 A. Biyadoo Island Resort: page 151 C. Danilo Cedrone / Futhuhul Bari: page 79 C. Angelo Cozzi / Gangemi: pages 23 B; 85 D; 87 D.The Crab: pages 85 E; 101 G; 104 B; 105 G; 113 F; 141 F. Mallio Falcioni / Mahureva: page 26 B. Flying Fish: page 19 C. Full Moon Beach Resort: page 26 D. Fun Island Vaadhoo: page 151 D. Giravaru Resort: page 27 F. Halaveli Holiday Village: page 87 C. Ihuru: page 26 A. Keyodhoo Felidu: page 114. Kurumba Village Resort: page 27 G,H. Laguna Beach Resort: page 151 F. Maafushivaru / Turisanda: page 85 C. Ranveli Resort: page 87 D. Seafari: pages 51 D,E; 83 F. Soneva Fushi / Baa Atoll: page 65 E. Thudufushi / The Crab: page 87 F.